Hard Conversations Unpacked

Hard Conversations Unpacked

The Whos, the Whens, and the What-Ifs

Jennifer Abrams

Foreword by Douglas Fisher and Nancy Frey

A Joint Publication

CORWIN
A SAGE Company

learningforward
THE PROFESSIONAL LEARNING ASSOCIATION

For information:

Corwin
A SAGE Company
2455 Teller Road
Thousand Oaks, California 91320
(800) 233-9936
www.corwin.com

SAGE Publications Ltd.
1 Oliver's Yard
55 City Road
London EC1Y 1SP
United Kingdom

SAGE Publications India Pvt. Ltd.
B 1/I 1 Mohan Cooperative Industrial Area
Mathura Road, New Delhi 110 044
India

SAGE Publications Asia-Pacific Pte. Ltd.
3 Church Street
#10-04 Samsung Hub
Singapore 049483

Program Director: Dan Alpert
Senior Associate Editor: Kimberly Greenberg
Editorial Assistant: Katie Crilley
Production Editor: Melanie Birdsall
Copy Editor: Terri Lee Paulsen
Typesetter: C&M Digitals (P) Ltd.
Proofreader: Catherine Forrest
Indexer: Molly Hall
Cover Designer: Candice Harman
Marketing Managers: Charline Maher and
                              Kimberly Kanakes

Printed in the United States of America

Library of Congress Cataloging-in-Publication Data

Names: Abrams, Jennifer, author.

Title: Hard conversations unpacked: The whos, the whens, and the what-ifs / Jennifer Abrams.

Description: Thousand Oaks, California : Corwin, a SAGE Company, [2016] |

Includes bibliographical references and index.

Identifiers: LCCN 2015035328 | ISBN 978-1-5063-0290-4 (pbk.: alk. paper)

Subjects: LCSH: Communication in education—United States. | Teachers' workshops—United States. | Educational leadership—United States.

Classification: LCC LB1033.5.A274 2016 | DDC 371.102/2—dc23 LC record available at http://lccn.loc.gov/2015035328

This book is printed on acid-free paper.

16 17 18 19 20 10 9 8 7 6 5 4 3 2 1

Contents

Foreword

Simply said, anyone who works in an organization with other people has to learn to have hard conversations. But we're not born with this skill. Oh, yes, we can have great conversations, dancing around the point, hoping that the listener will infer our message and make changes. It happens to all of us, and often. Not too long ago, a teacher friend of ours told us about a colleague (let's call her Amanda) who was new to their grade level. Amanda didn't establish or communicate clear learning intentions for her students in her lessons. As a result, Amanda's students were not sure what it was they were supposed to learn, much less why they would be learning that, and so they regularly performed below the grade-level average.

We asked our friend what she said to Amanda. Her response: "It's not my job to talk with her about this. That's the principal's job. I keep my nose out of it." And therein lines the problem. A common response to problematic situations is avoidance. We don't have honest conversations with our colleagues because we don't think it's our job, or because that person might get mad at us, or because we're not sure how.

As we processed this situation with our friend, we encouraged her to talk with her colleague about the situation and how to resolve it. We believe that people show up to work to do the best job they know how. It's just that there may be things missing. Our friend decided to have the conversation with Amanda. Here's what we learned: "Oh, we had a great conversation. I told her about my planning process. You know, I plan after my kids go to bed. And I showed her some of the tools that I have found that really help me create strong lessons, lessons with a clear purpose. I talked about how much my students like the class and how they perform at least at our grade-level average, if not above. But you know what? She hasn't changed." And why would she? Amanda probably thought she was having a friendly conversation with a peer and was likely not aware of the issue, at least as perceived from the perspective of our friend. Rather than avoid the conversation this time, our friend made inferences but was not direct enough for anything to change.

Thankfully, our friend did not engage an aggressive conversation. These occur when people are very frustrated, often at their wit's end. They make threats, demands, and come across as rude and uncaring. Imagine saying to Amada, a hard-working teacher trying to engage her students in meaningful learning, the following: "I expect that you have a learning target every day for every lesson. If not, I will start the documentation process to have you removed from the classroom." WOW—Amanda will wonder what hit her. She'll likely become defensive, unable to listen to the conversation. Further, this aggressive conversation will not offer Amanda any advice about how to address the concerns that were raised.

That's not to say that no one engages in behaviors that require that immediate attention, and may result in their termination. But most of the time, if we want people to change their behaviors, we need a different kind of conversation. In the language of Jennifer Abrams, these hard conversations are designed to be *humane and growth producing.* And this is key, and why we like this book so much. All of us can benefit from learning how to have this type of conversation. It's a type of conversation that is all too rare, unfortunately. But the good news is that it can be learned.

Since reading *Hard Conversations Unpacked,* we have noticed that the tenets in this book can be applied to conversations with students, colleagues, employees, supervisors, friends, family, and yes, even spouses. We can learn to have conversations that provide others with information about the problem, why it's a problem, and what we recommend be done about it. Importantly, these conversations are not monologues; they're an opportunity to dialogue and reach a better understanding.

In this book, Abrams updates her process for planning a hard conversation. She also provides clear and succinct advice about engaging in hard conversations. Again, our biggest takeaway from her book is the idea that these conversations must be humane and growth producing. She reminds readers that people have to be prepared for these conversations, and offers a tool to help people plan their conversations. Although that seems counter to the idea of a dialogue, we can attest to the fact that it works. Both of us use her tool to plan important conversations and are consistently pleased with the results.

Therefore, we encouraged our friend to have a hard conversation with Amanda. She started with a reassuring statement ("I really enjoy working with you; you have a lot of creative ideas that have helped me."). She then named the issue ("I am concerned that your students don't always know what they're supposed to learn, or why."). She provided an example from a recent lesson and then offered some examples of the impact this has had ("You told me that your students aren't performing as well as you expect. The lesson we reviewed in our collaborative team didn't have a learning intention so maybe they learned some other things, but not what you wanted them to learn."). And then, our friend opened up the conversation, which we're told was rich. Amanda asked for help, recognizing that the standards for this grade level were unfamiliar to her. She said that she chose not to communicate her expectations because she was afraid that they were too low. Now they were ready to take action and make a difference in the lives of students.

We chose the example of Amanda to reinforce a point. Our friend and Amanda were peers. This process works beautifully for administrators as well, but imagine the impact on the organization if every person felt comfortable having humane, growth-producing conversations. We all deserve the opportunity to grow and develop. In doing so, we will make mistakes. We will disagree with others. But we can learn from those situations when we know that people care enough to engage us in dialogue.

—*Douglas Fisher and Nancy Frey*

Preface

Live courage, breathe courage, give courage.

—Dhan Gopal

WHAT IS A HARD CONVERSATION?

Hard conversations come in all forms. They range from a formal evaluation conference in which you tell someone they need to improve, to the briefest comment about behavior at a team meeting; from a colleague-to-colleague discussion in the parking lot, to the rollout of a district initiative that prompts resistance. Hard conversations occur between colleagues, with administrators, at team meetings, and with any adult connected to the school. The content can be teacher or administrator behavior, lack of follow-through, not meeting performance expectations, responding to a challenging communication, or about so many other "goings on" that happen in schools. Whenever you feel uncomfortable or fearful, have second thoughts, or avoid saying something, you are circling a hard conversation.

WHY A SECOND BOOK ABOUT A SIMILAR TOPIC?

Since I wrote the book *Having Hard Conversations* in 2009, I have had the opportunity to learn from people around the globe. I have researched the topic more deeply, discovered more nuance in the work. I have seen up close and personal the difficulty of having conversations that are both humane and growth producing. I have been on a worthwhile journey, conversation by conversation, in which I uncovered so much more to share with readers.

I have engaged with this new learning supported by the most recent research on the need for professional and social capital among educators in order to increase student achievement (Hargreaves & Fullan, 2012). And I'm even more convinced of the critical need for generative, collegial communication for the sake of our profession. The teacher evaluation initiatives that have come to the fore in the last five years are but an indication of how urgently we require the skill to have hard conversations that facilitate professional growth as well as results in classrooms.

In the eight years since the publication of *Having Hard Conversations* (Abrams, 2009), participants in my workshops have asked me questions

I didn't address and to which I didn't have answers. A lot of "what ifs?" came up, such as:

- How to deal with difficult feedback

- What to do if you cry

- How to respond if someone starts to yell or make a certain statement

Parts in this book were written in response to those requests as I sought to incorporate new learnings on how to shape a hard conversation so it is both thoughtful and substantive, skillful and compassionate.

In addition, this work includes topics that weren't addressed in the previous book:

- How to have hard conversations with supervisors

- How to have hard conversations with groups versus individuals

- How organizational dynamics play a part in a hard conversation

- How the filters of gender, race, and generation can be factors to consider in the conflict one is facing

WHO IS THIS BOOK FOR? ALL OF US

Since starting the workshops, I have heard from classroom teachers in K–12, employees in custodial services, food services, the business office, secretaries, and instructional aides and others without what they consider to be "positional authority." They aren't comfortable having hard conversations. They tell me, "This isn't my job. The person who makes the big bucks, has a door to her office and has a business card needs to speak up. I don't get paid enough to have these types of conversations."

I respectfully disagree. If you are an adult working in a school, from the custodian to the secretary in the main office, from the aide to the department chair, you are modeling for the students what it means to be a professional. So, this book is for you—not just for your supervisor. We all need to have a sense of collective responsibility to learn how to speak professionally in our workplaces. We all need to learn how to speak up skillfully around what matters. No one is off the hook. The students are watching us.

DO YOU NEED TO HAVE READ *HAVING HARD CONVERSATIONS* TO READ THIS BOOK? NO

This book includes coverage of two key tools from my first book, the *outcome map* for action planning and the *foundational script* for the initial parts of the conversation itself. Many of the new learnings presented in the book build on the coverage of these tools. I have re-explained both tools chapters in sufficient depth to make readers comfortable using the tools without having read the first book. No worries. I've got you covered.

HOW DOES THIS BOOK WORK?

Like my previous book on the same topic, this book follows the preparation of a hard conversation, from preplanning to scripting to dealing with responses to the conversation.

Chapter 1 asks, "Is this really a hard conversation or some other type of conversation?" Is this a "cease and desist" conversation? Is this a clarifying conversation? Or is this really this type of a hard conversation? This chapter will assist you in placing the hard conversation in a frame to determine which type of conversation you are having.

Chapter 2 looks at, "If this is a hard conversation, what do I need to do to keep the conversation from becoming too emotional?" We are trying to make sure that the conversation stays in the zone of the cognitive. If we have gone too "affective"—started hitting below the belt, or moved from behavior to personality, we need to bring ourselves back to the professional.

Chapter 3 asks us to go through the outcome map with an emphasis on what is going on for the other person in this situation. This deeper dive into the action planning and preparation focuses on the "other." Being other-focused helps us stay empathic and thoughtful during the planning of the hard conversation and assists us in understanding what might be going on from the other person's perspective.

Chapter 4 asks us to consider, "What else do I need to be mindful of as I prepare for the conversation and how do I consider the context in which the conversation will take place? What are the politics and 'covert processes' at play in the school, district, or organization, and how might those inform and impact the hard conversation?" There is always a bigger picture in which we are working. How can you go "macro" in scope and see how this hard conversation fits into a bigger dynamic? How does this new perspective help you talk effectively to supervisors or groups as well?

Chapter 5 brings us to the question, "How one can speak in the most humane and growth-producing way possible?" This is where the foundational script and all the additional nuances are found. We will be using David Rock's work on threat and reward, his SCARF model, to add some language to create a less threatening start to the conversation.

Chapter 6 is about "What if I need to address (fill in the blank)? And what do I do if they say (fill in the blank)?" These questions have been asked to me by countless participants in workshops, and while I don't have an exact answer, I have some ideas of how you can be more prepared to respond when challenging questions are posed.

Chapter 7 gives responses to the question, "How can I prepare psychologically for being the recipient of 'hard' feedback?" As we have prepared to be deliverers of challenging feedback, we also need to ready ourselves to be recipients of some difficult commentary. How does one manage oneself in those situations? These strategies might assist you in handling yourself with more grace.

"The Conversation Continues." At the end of every chapter, there will be a section entitled "The Conversation Continues . . ." In that section I will provide references to books and resources for further study on the chapter topics.

REMIND ME: WHY DO I NEED TO HAVE A HARD CONVERSATION?

U.S. Congressman and esteemed social justice advocate John Lewis was interviewed by a high school senior asking for advice about going into his adulthood. Congressman Lewis, without hesitation, responded: "What I wish for your life is that you get into trouble. Necessary trouble." I take Congressman Lewis's advice and try to live it out in the work I do. We need to speak up for the field, advocate for the democratic ideals on which our profession was based, speak for students who don't have a voice, for the best teaching possible for all students, for the professional cultures we deserve to work in and for the next generation of educators. We need to get into necessary trouble.

At the beginning of my teaching, I was fearful of hard conversations. I didn't find them exciting or easy. They still aren't comfortable, but I find almost three decades later that they are even more necessary. I want to suggest that we as educators can study them from the balcony as an important and essential part of our work and our professional growth, and get more skilled in speaking up. Let's learn together.

Acknowledgments

Much appreciation goes to the following people who taught me how to be more "other-focused." I am grateful.

To those school boards, school districts, and organizations who pushed this work forward and gave me opportunities to test-run the content: Judy Levinsohn and her new teacher mentors and new administrator candidates at the Orange County Office of Education; Judi Gottschalk and Kay Coleman at iLeadAZ; Mary Gomes and members of the Association of California School Administrators (ACSA); the Independent Schools Association of the Central States (ISACS); the administrators at Mountain View High School who kept asking me, "What if?"; Doug Fisher, Nancy Frey, Ian Pumpian, and the Health Sciences Middle and High School faculty; the nurses and employees of Community Hospital of the Monterey Peninsula and Stanford Hospital and Clinics who helped me see how this work connects in a hospital setting; Kevin Silberberg, superintendent, and Lauri Heffernan, union president, at Panama-Buena Vista, SD, who came together to see that both sides of the negotiation table should have this skill set; to the Maine Women Administrators Group and Windham Primary School in Windham, Maine, who showed me coaching on this topic via Skype and Google Hangout is doable and worthwhile; to Kehillah Jewish High School and Hausner Day School who, along with Catholic educators in Canada, brought a faith-based perspective to the work; and to those at Learning Forward conferences who participated in the workshops and shaped my thinking.

To my international colleagues who pushed me to look at my American filter around this work: Suzanne Molitor, Susan Adamthwaite, Hilda Pierorazio, Rob Lebovsky, and so many others in Peel DSB in Mississauga, Ontario, Canada; Luciana Cardarelli and the Catholic Principals Council of Ontario; Aggie Nemes at Toronto CDSB; Dick Krajzar and members of the East Asia Regional Council of Schools (EARCOS); David and Elaine Brownlow and Gavin Grift at Hawker-Brownlow in Australia; and Colleen Douglas and Janine Remnant at Massey University in New Zealand. This work has deepened and broadened thanks to your perspectives.

To my friends and family: my father, Richard Abrams; my late mother, Myrna Abrams; my brother and sister-in-law, Adam and Shelley Abrams; and nephews, Joe and Evan. My friends and colleagues, Jen Wakefield, Greg Matza, Ann Idzik, John Hebert, John Fredrich, Sean O'Maonaigh, Nancy Goldstein, Sharon Ofek, Becki Cohn-Vargas, Peter DeWitt, and Jeffrey Benson.

To my extreme self-care support team: Isidro Pimentel, Pam Lund, Mary Ruth Quinn, Josh Edick, Bobbi Emel, Laurence Collins, Tamara Vinokurova, Bill

Weihman, and Suki Paulovitz who made it easy for me to focus on the work and did the magic behind the scenes.

To my editor, Dan Alpert, and the fabulous folks at Corwin who listened to my voice and have promoted and encouraged my work from the beginning: Kristin Anderson, Mayan McDermott, Taryn Williams, Lisa Shaw, Kim Greenberg, Elena Nikitina, Monique Corridori, and Mike Soules. Dancing with you has been a treat.

PUBLISHER'S ACKNOWLEDGMENTS

Corwin would like to thank the following individuals for their editorial insight and guidance:

Virginia E. Kelsen
Executive Director, College and Careers
Chaffey Joint Union High School District

Roseanne Lopez
Chief Academic Officer, Elementary Education
Amphitheater School District

Charles Lowery
Assistant Professor
Ohio University

Tanna Nicely
Principal
South Knoxville Elementary

David Vernot
Curriculum Consultant
Butler County Educational Service Center

About the Author

 A former high school English teacher, new teacher coach, and professional developer for Palo Alto Unified School District (Palo Alto, CA), **Jennifer Abrams** is now an international educational and communications consultant for public and independent schools, hospitals, universities, and nonprofits. Jennifer trains and coaches educators, hospital personnel, and others on new employee support, supervision, being generationally savvy, having hard conversations, and effective collaboration skills.

In her educational consulting work, Jennifer has presented at annual conferences sponsored by Learning Forward, ASCD, NASSP, NAESP, AMLE, ISACS, and the New Teacher Center, as well as at international conferences led by EARCOS, NESA, TAISI, ACAMIS, and the Teachers' and Principals' Centers for International School Leadership. Jennifer's communications consulting in the health care sector includes work at the Community Hospital of the Monterey Peninsula and Stanford Hospital.

Jennifer's publications include *Having Hard Conversations* and *The Multigenerational Workplace: Communicate, Collaborate, and Create Community*; a chapter in Art Costa and Bena Kallick's book, *Learning and Leading With Habits of Mind: 16 Essential Characteristics for Success*; and her contribution to the book *Mentors in the Making: Developing New Leaders for New Teachers*, published by Teachers College Press. Jennifer writes a monthly newsletter, "Voice Lessons," available for reading at and subscribing to on her website, www.jenniferabrams.com.

Jennifer has been recognized as one of "18 Women All K–12 Educators Need to Know" by *Education Week*'s *Finding Common Ground* blog and has been a featured interviewee for ASCD's video series, *Master Class*, and the Ontario Ministry of Education for their *Leadership Matters: Supporting Open-to-Learning Conversations* video series.

Jennifer considers herself a "voice coach," helping others learn how to best use their voices—be it collaborating on a team, presenting in front of an audience, coaching a colleague, supervising an employee, or in any situation where it is imperative to speak up around what matters. Jennifer can be reached at jennifer@jenniferabrams.com, www.jenniferabrams.com, and on Twitter @jenniferabrams.

Our conversations invent us. Through our speech and our silence, we become smaller or larger selves. Through our speech and our silence, we diminish or enhance the other person, and we narrow or expand the possibilities between us. How we use our voice determines the quality of our relationships, who we are in the world, and what the world can be and might become. Clearly, a lot is at stake here.

—Harriet Lerner, *The Dance of Connection*

Is This Really a Hard Conversation or Something Else? 1

Nothing important comes with instructions.

—James Richardson

QUESTIONS TO ASK YOURSELF AT THE BEGINNING OF THIS PROCESS

Something doesn't feel right. Something isn't going well. It isn't "working." It might not have been okay for some time. And, now is the time to speak up. So you think. But take pause. Before you jump into a hard conversation, here are a few questions to ask yourself. Ask yourself these questions as a checklist, perhaps— in order to place a "sandbox" around the challenge so you know it is truly a hard conversation as is described in this book, and not something else.

Is this something that is actually illegal, unethical? Is this behavior harming children? Is the action unlawful or going against policy of the school or district?

If an employee is drinking on the job, or texting children in an inappropriate way (sexually or being overly personal), or stealing, for example, those behaviors are *beyond* the type of hard conversation discussed in this book. If illegal or unethical actions are being taken, one needs to contact supervisors, human resources, or another appropriate organization. In these scenarios, the conversation that needs to take place is a "cease and desist" conversation or a "thank you, you are done here" conversation. Safety is at risk. These types of conversations aren't discussed in this book, but they are critical to have. Seek assistance. This book addresses *other* types of conversations.

What about hard conversations with individuals with mental illness or employees with dementia? Those suspected of being in an emotional state that is unstable and unsafe for students to be around? Those conversations are *also* beyond the boundaries of this book and need to be handled by those who have the expertise to manage the conversations in a humane, professional, and appropriate manner. Know who to go to when things grow beyond your purview. HR offices often know where to go in these cases.

Is this actually a clarifying conversation and not a hard conversation?

"Clarity First, Accountability Follows" Blog for *Education Week*

http://blogs.edweek.org/edweek/finding_common_ground/2014/08/clarity_first_accountability_follows.html

One of my favorite quotes of all time with regard to hard conversations work is from Blaine Lee. He says, "Almost all conflict is the result of violated expectations." The question I always ask is, "Does the other person know the expectations?" If so, then, if the expectations were violated, we could choose to move to a hard conversation. If not, a clarifying conversation needs to come first.

We so often think we have been clear. We should be able to speak up and judge and express ourselves. Again, take pause. Did we *actually* make it clear what is and isn't part of the work? Did the job descriptions get reviewed this school year? Have we revisited the group norms for how we work together? With new positions in our schools, often with coaching roles or teacher on special assignment roles, we write at the bottom of the job description a phrase such as "other duties as assigned," and that part of the description grows ever bigger as the year moves on, but true clarification of what those duties were never happened. Not good.

I worked with one new principal who was frustrated that the team leaders at his middle school "weren't doing their jobs" until he discovered there was never a job description written. And so what did it mean to "not do your job"? Fuzzy.

We need to be "two feet in the present" with our work, and clarifying conversations need to take place before hard conversations. Clarity before accountability.

Don't Use "Fuzzy" Words
Don't presume you and your colleagues have the same definitions for the following words or many others. Articulate what you mean. Prepare, Early, Professional, Engage, Inform, Communicate, Practice, Team Player, Initiative, Leadership, Timely, Connect

Is this a problem that can be solved or a polarity that needs to be managed?

We think we have many problems in our schools today. For example, a teacher is not "following" the curriculum. He is labeled a "renegade" or a "cowboy." Perhaps he needs alignment with the curriculum timeline, but does that mean we don't value his autonomy in other choices that he makes? I bet in this case as in many others in schools we aren't dealing with a problem that is solvable but a polarity that needs to be managed. In this situation, we aren't completely against autonomy in all ways; we just want a little more alignment in this one way.

Polarities are prominent in many of the debates and conflicts we have in our schools today. Should we focus on the social-emotional needs of students or the academic needs of students? Should we care about getting things done or care about the people who are doing the work? It isn't an either-or. Like inhaling and exhaling (you can't do one without the other), polarities are interdependent. They cannot be totally one-sided. Instead of getting too indignant and pushing your heels in on your side of the argument, realize there is no problem to be solved because in fact, we are facing a polarity that needs to be *managed*. Perhaps someone has "gone off the bubble" in one direction or another and needs to find more of a balance, but we cannot assume we can have one hard conversation and all will be solved. Some things are just not solvable. Just as we need to inhale and exhale and can't do one without the other, knowing the difference between a polarity and a problem will help you to better understand the challenge ahead.

Jane Kise is a master at untangling the challenges we face and determining if they are solvable problems or manageable polarities. Kise's work *Unleashing the Positive Power of Differences: Polarity Thinking in Our Schools* is an excellent book that "provides tools and processes for avoiding those pendulum swings by listening to the wisdom of multiple points of view" (Kise, 2014, p. 2). Look at the text box below to see if you are actually trying to solve something with a hard conversation that is truly unsolvable and needs some additional discussion in order to be better managed instead.

Common Polarities in Education

Not either-or but "Yes, and":

- Autonomy and collaboration
- Team relationships and team tasks
- Clarity and flexibility
- Continuity and change
- Conditional respect and unconditional respect
- Work priorities and home priorities
- Needs of students and needs of staff
- Teacher as lecturer and teacher as facilitator
- Centralization and decentralization
- School responsibility and social responsibility

—From *Unleashing the Positive Power of Differences: Polarity Thinking in Our Schools,* Jane Kise (2014)

Is this *my* conversation to have or should someone else be having it?

You might find yourself thinking, "I personally need to handle this." And you could be right. *You* do need to take action. The question is to whom should you be speaking. Instead of talking directly to the individual you think you should be talking to might you need to be talking to someone else? Do you need to have a hard conversation *up?*

Co-presenting with a director, higher up than myself within the hierarchy of the school district, I often struggled with extensive absences of members of our team at our meetings. Was it my conversation to have with those team members or was it the director, who was higher up in the hierarchy than myself, who should have those conversations? She had more "pull" than I did. Sometimes it is someone above you with whom you need to speak, not the person you initially wanted to address. Sometimes you discover a bigger conversation happening across the organization and whatever you wanted to talk about is actually a systemic problem. Something hasn't been clarified from above. It doesn't mean you shouldn't speak up. The question is to whom.

Should I have a coaching conversation instead of a hard conversation? Is this conversation one in which to use humble inquiry instead?

Edgar Schein, author of *Humble Inquiry: The Gentle Art of Asking Instead of Telling* (2013) and *Helping: How to Offer, Give, and Receive Help* (2009), observes that many of us in higher-status roles often default to telling or into "confrontational inquiry." Instead of speaking so directly, consider being "here and now humble" and put yourself in a vulnerable place, admitting dependency on the other and shifting to a truly curious space that brings you to a space of questioning, not *addressing.* Admittedly, our task-oriented, high-speed culture of accomplishment seems incongruent with slowing down and "getting curious," but if you think sitting down as equals and asking honest questions might lead to the outcome you hope for, you could consider inquiry instead of a hard conversation.

These are not the only questions to ask yourself before you continue with the planning of a hard conversation, but they are good ones to consider. I always consider defaulting to coaching, curiosity, and question asking as my go-to communication style.

Yet, if something is

- educationally unsound,

- physically unsafe, or

- emotionally damaging,

and you think a conversation with declarative sentences versus question asking would be best, then move forward with planning this type of hard conversation.

There are so many types of conversation to have, so be sure you know which one to start with. See below for a visual representation of where a hard conversation could fall in the scheme of all types of conversations.

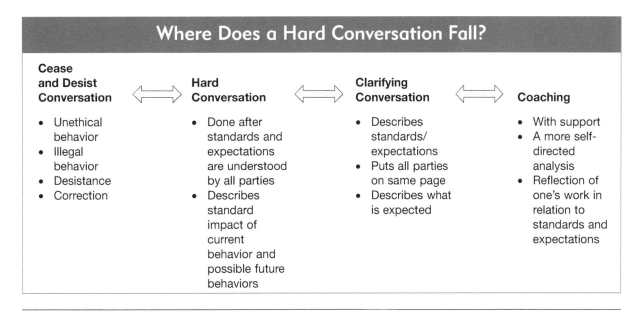

Where Does a Hard Conversation Fall?			
Cease and Desist Conversation ⟸⟹	**Hard Conversation** ⟸⟹	**Clarifying Conversation** ⟸⟹	**Coaching**
• Unethical behavior • Illegal behavior • Desistance • Correction	• Done after standards and expectations are understood by all parties • Describes standard impact of current behavior and possible future behaviors	• Describes standards/ expectations • Puts all parties on same page • Describes what is expected	• With support • A more self-directed analysis • Reflection of one's work in relation to standards and expectations

Note: There is no single direction for having conversations correctly. One can move back and forth on the continuum as needed.

THE CONVERSATION CONTINUES . . .

Helping: How to Offer, Give, and Receive Help by Edgar H. Schein, Berrett-Koehler Publishers, 2009

Humble Inquiry: The Gentle Art of Asking Instead of Telling by Edgar H. Schein, Berrett-Koehler Publishers, 2013

Unleashing the Positive Power of Our Differences: Polarity Thinking in Our Schools by Jane A. G. Kise, Corwin, 2014

Clarity, Clarity, Clarity 2

You're not disappointed in what it is. You're disappointed in what you thought it would be.

—Unknown

They're wrong. We're right. But, were we? In Chapter 1 I spoke to the fact that clarity before accountability is essential. We should not have a hard conversation before we have been clear about our expectations. The idea of being clear with one's expectations is one of the most challenging concepts to follow *in practice.* Easy to say. Not so easy to do. Before we have hard conversations and hold people accountable for their actions. In both one-on-one professional relationships (i.e., co-teaching) and in group relationships (i.e., teams, departments, whole faculty, whole district) it is essential to step back and articulate what we agree to in terms of how we will work together. Then when we have a hard conversation, we have already articulated and agreed to what we are talking about as a challenge arises. This chapter will speak to

- the clarity of public agreements as a proactive step,
- keeping things cognitive so we don't become unprofessional and emotional in our hard conversations, and
- "walking our talk" and behaving professionally in the workplace.

THE NEED FOR PUBLIC AGREEMENTS

In schools, students are often the ones with whom we are clearest. We know young people need specifics in terms of how to behave and interact. Windham Primary School in Windham, Maine, has some very clear ideas of how students are to behave on the playground. Beyond "Be safe, be respectful, and be responsible," they go into specific detail. A few examples from their one-page poster include:

- Go down the slides on your bottom. Feet first. One at a time.
- Go in one direction on the overhead climbers. Start on the side closest to the school.

- If someone falls off the merry-go-round, please stop and let them get back on.

- Everyone faces the school on the swings. Keep your bottom on the seat.

While most everyone agrees with the principle of articulating norms for those who are *attending* school, many colleagues scoff at the idea of creating norms for those of us *working in* schools. After all, we are adults. Rules are patronizing and as professionals we certainly don't need to be "spoon-fed."

Bob Kegan and Lisa Laskow Lahey, in their book *How the Way We Talk Can Change the Way We Work: Seven Languages for Transformation,* speak to the need for public agreements. "The ongoing practice of a language of public agreement is a route to nurturing a direct experience of organizational integrity" (Kegan & Lahey, 2001, pp. 112–113). *Organizational integrity* strikes me as a great term.

I think many of us have been in a situation where our expectations haven't been clearly articulated. We then complain that the other person isn't being "mature" or "professional," or "adult" when we actually need to step back and reframe our conversations into *public agreements*. We have laws; we have policies; we have contracts. We have standards, job expectations, and benchmarks. Adults manage quite well with this type of wording and framing. Public agreements are one more way to speak to our ways of working together, and they keep things cognitive instead of moving us to the emotional. Many of us appreciate clarity and certainty. (More on this later.) The speaking aloud of these types of agreements helps us all to be "two feet in the present."

The Language of Public Agreement

The ongoing practice of a language of public agreement is a route to nurturing a direct experience of organizational integrity. But it is important to notice that this does not come about through some naïve belief that because everyone holds hands and agrees to something, it removes forever after, like a magic wand, all offending behavior. Not at all. . . . But notice that it is only because of the existence of a public agreement that there [are violations].

—From *How the Way We Talk Can Change the Way We Work,* Robert Kegan and Lisa Lahey (2001), pp. 112–113

Victor ESD Basics

Victor Elementary School District (VESD), in Victorville, California, supplies pocket reminders to employees of their district agreements. Some carry these in purses or wallets. These agreements (Victor Elementary School District, 2005) were written more than a decade ago but "live" in the district beyond the pocket reminder and into the life of meetings and all interactions.

The VESD Basics

1. Everything we do will advance our Vision, Mission, and Motto, which shall be known, owned, and energized by all.

2. The VESD Promise to Employees is our principle belief. It will be honored by everyone.

3. The Professional Guidelines for Common Courtesy are the standards for our conduct.

4. Meeting Guidelines serve as norms for all meetings.

5. We are ambassadors of the Victor Elementary School District. We speak positively about the district and each other at work and in the community.

6. We take personal responsibility for personal and group decisions; therefore, "We Versus They" does not exist, we do not blame or make excuses.

7. Everyone has a responsibility to communicate concerns and possible solutions to the appropriate person—the appropriate person will ensure follow-through to resolution. Seek a solution rather than a "rule book" response.

8. Give people your full attention—"Be There." Always recognize each other immediately with eye contact, a smile, and their name whenever possible, using greetings such as, "Good Morning," "How may I help you?" "I would be happy to," "Have you been helped?

9. We return all calls or e-mails in a timely manner (phone calls within 3 rings, e-mails within 24 hours).

10. We are always Ladies and Gentlemen in all interactions, even when a conversation grows abusive and must be terminated.

11. It is our responsibility to participate as a team member in a collaborative environment using ideas, resources, and information to achieve common goals.

12. Think well of yourself and take pride in your professional dress, personal appearance, and personal health.

COGNITIVE VERSUS AFFECTIVE CONFLICT

We all aim to keep our conflicts and hard conversations at a cognitive level. We all try to stay professional and mature in our interactions and not become overly emotional in our responses in tense situations. Public agreements can help in doing so. Yet, when things get "corrupted"—when our expectations haven't been articulated, and we when devolve to unhealthy responses—chances are we have moved into affective conflict. We have gone past simmering and we boil over, we go for the jugular, we overpersonalize, we throw in emotionally laden adjectives; it gets "bad." We are not our best selves at moments such as these.

Robert Garmston, in his book *Unlocking Group Potential to Improve Schools*, writes,

> Affective conflict lowers team effectiveness by fostering hostility, distrust, cynicism, avoidance, and apathy among team members. This type of conflict focuses on personalized anger or resentment, usually directed at specific individuals rather than ideas. It often emerges when C-type [cognitive] conflict becomes corrupted because members lack the skills or norms to disagree gracefully. In such settings, disagreement about ideas can become personalized. (Garmston, 2012, p. 107)

So what we are working toward in our conversation isn't a conversation that is so light it doesn't have some disagreement in it, but that the disagreement stays cognitive; the disagreement is about substantive differences of opinion. C-type conflict conversations can "improve team effectiveness and produce better decisions, increased commitment, increased cohesiveness, increased empathy, and increased understanding. Such cognitive conflict is a natural part of a properly functioning team" (Garmston, 2012, pp. 107–108). We aren't trying to not disagree. That isn't good for the group, and it is unrealistic. In the text box below are examples of when someone has not stayed cognitive. Imagine the emotionally triggered responses to statements such as these. We need to stop speaking in these ways and causing affective conflict.

What *Not* to Say: A-Type Conflict Starters

- "Your life is a train wreck."
- "You are toxic to our team."
- "You are poison."
- "You're a mess."
- "Man up."
- "Stop being such a cry baby."
- "You are such a drama queen."
- "Why are you such a pain to work with?"
- "You have always been such a stickler for the rules. You 'army sergeant.'"

RELATIONAL TRUST MATTERS

Affective conflict can be wounding and dangerous in schools long term. Someone says, "Grow up," or "Get over it," or "Stop being so sensitive," and the drama begins. It sticks in the craws of individuals for a long time and student achievement suffers. It might not sound like a big deal—just a few words—but those words can have long-term effects. We need to figure out how to not go "affective." Research tells us relational trust is pivotal to student growth. Saying hello in the front office as you come into work every day leads to student growth. Truly.

Let me "thread the needle" on that statement. If we have respectful interactions as our baseline and demonstrate an ability to do our job, our colleagues will see our competence and our kindness and respond accordingly. When they notice our professionalism and trust us, they listen to us. And, then perhaps something we suggest or share might influence their practice for the better. They hear a good strategy, they try it, and students benefit. When colleagues ignore each other, or grumble or sigh in communications with each other, no one can get past those behaviors to share their best practices. Relational trust among colleagues matters.

"[A] broad base of trust across a school community lubricates much of the school's day-to-day functioning and is a critical resource as local leaders embark on ambitious improvement plans" (Bryk & Schneider, 2002, p. 5). Bryk and Schneider contend that schools with a high degrees of "relational trust" are far more likely to make the kinds of changes that help raise student achievement than those where relations are poor (Gordon, 2002).

What does relational trust look like? Bryk and Schneider (2002) speak to four vital signs for identifying and assessing trust.

1. **Respect**—Do we acknowledge one another's dignity and ideas? Do we interact in a courteous way?

2. **Competence**—Do we believe in each other's ability and willingness to fulfill our responsibilities effectively?

3. **Personal regard**—Do we care about each other personally and professionally? Are we willing to go beyond our formal roles and responsibilities to go the extra mile?

4. **Integrity**—Can we trust each other to put the interests of students first, especially when tough decisions have to be made? Do we keep our word?

In the spirit of clarity, it might be helpful for a school staff to speak to the behaviors that *embody* trust. A self-assessment of relational trust could include:

- Do I "show up"? Show up on time or late?

- Do I know, understand, respect, and follow the learning outcomes/course descriptions of my classes? If so, how? Follow the objectives for the department? The goals of the school?

- If asked to complete some paperwork or attend a meeting on behalf of the department or do some work for the team, do I get it done?

- Do I look like I enjoy teaching? Enjoy the school? Enjoy my colleagues? If so, how?

- Do I communicate with parents in a timely fashion? If so, how?

- Do I hold myself to a high standard for what I do and produce? If so, how?

- Am I aware of the school values, norms, and the way the school sees itself? Do I work well within those values? If so, how? Do I embody them or just give them lip service?

- Do I show consideration for the feelings of others? (E.g., say "Hello," "Thank you," "I'm sorry," "What can I do to help?")

- Do I gossip? Talk poorly of colleagues in front of others or to students?

- Am I able to stand outside myself and see how I might be impacting others or be seen by others? If so, how?

- If I am given feedback, do I listen to it and react appropriately, changing behavior if necessary? If so, how?

- Am I open to hearing all perspectives? If so, how? And when hearing all perspectives, do I honor them or shut down?

- Do I cooperate with special education staff, counselors, or administrators so that services are provided to the students? Do I fill out the progress reports and do the required/suggested accommodations with a positive attitude?

- Do I manage my anxiety in a way that is appropriate, not yelling at or crying in front of all staff or students?

- Do I know of the hierarchy of positions in the school? Do I know where to go for the appropriate person for the appropriate concern? Do I look for solutions rather than sit with the problem and complain in the parking lot?

- Do I want to work in a group, and do I show that through my body language, contributions, and attitude?

- Do I show an ability to listen for understanding and empathy?

- Do I manage impulsivity or interrupt more often than not, inserting my point of view?

- Do I use positive presuppositions when coming together with a given group—presuming positive intention and potential?

- Do I seem to have a sense of humor? Can I laugh at myself?

- Do I have a sense of personal space, body language, and appropriate sense of decorum in a given setting? With both adults and students?

- Am I aware that I am not allowing equitable participation by talking too much at meetings or talking too little and not contributing?

In the end, we can't define *every* behavior that we would like to see as we collaborate together in schools. Yet, schools often err on the side of being fuzzy in articulating what they would like to see in interactions among the adults in the workplace. Trust is built by living out the behaviors above; *and*, without being our best adult selves, trust doesn't grow.

"BUT . . ."

Many comments surface in workshops I facilitate when I encourage participants to work on clarity before accountability.

"Isn't clarity just another word for being too rules based, too authoritarian?"

"Isn't this public agreement 'thing' culturally 'relative'?"

"I just feel uncomfortable with clarity. I think it is code for being mean."

All of the comments and questions above are valid concerns. And, I disagree that clarity connotes meanness. Tone is everything. Purpose is everything. There is a rationale for why we have public agreements. Organizational beliefs about how adults interact with one another have been created for the sake of students. Public agreements aren't designed to create a top-down, "Big Brother is watching," type of culture. Clarity assists us in understanding what behaviors are best suited for a specific environment and supporting one another in doing important work.

And culture always matters. Peoria, Illinois; Staten Island, New York; and Temecula, California, are different places in which to learn and work, as are Ho Chi Minh City, Vietnam, and Cape Town, South Africa. All the more reason to promote greater clarity through public agreement.

THE CONVERSATION CONTINUES . . .

The Adaptive School: A Sourcebook for Developing Collaborative Groups by Robert Garmston and Bruce Wellman, Christopher Gordon Publishers, 1999

How the Way We Talk Can Change the Way We Work by Robert Kegan and Lisa Laskow Lahey, Jossey-Bass, 2001

Trust in Schools: A Core Resource for Improvement by Anthony Bryk and Barbara Schneider, American Sociological Association's Rose Series in Sociology by Russell Sage Foundation, 2002

Being Other-Focused 3
Planning the Hard Conversation

What you see and what I tell you isn't even half the story.

—Unknown

Despite your repeated efforts to provide clarity, you will, at times, be misinterpreted. Public agreements aren't kept, norms are violated, coaching doesn't create change, and a hard conversation is on the horizon.

After we acknowledge that we cannot avoid speaking up, and, after taking a few deep breaths, our next best response to these situations is *to think before we speak.* It isn't easy especially when we encounter unanticipated events. People walk into your office. You walk unexpectedly into a situation and someone's temper is flaring. We cannot control all interactions. *Yet,* when we can, we should always try to get our words right.

Managing our impulsivity is doable (three deep breaths, everyone) and finding the appropriate words is possible.

PLANNING AHEAD

Robert Garmston and Bruce Wellman (1999), in their book *The Adaptive School: A Sourcebook for Developing Collaborative Groups,* share a terrific thinking process titled an Outcome Map.

Humane and growth-producing conversations, ones that are skillful and compassionate, have at their outset an outcome they head toward. They aren't done off the cuff, without thought, or driven by a gut response. They are as thoughtful and kind as can be possible at the time.

Beyond acknowledging a need for a change and requesting a new behavior, we should try our best, through both our language and our nonverbals, to indicate we want to keep the relationship intact. It takes forethought, generosity, and skill to do it all. The Outcome Map template helps us with this process.

Thinking through answers to the following six questions, which are articulated in full in *Having Hard Conversations* (Abrams, 2009), is a terrific beginning to that thinking process.

The six questions in an Outcome Map are

1. What is the presenting problem?

2. What is the tentative outcome?

3. What are specific desired behaviors connected to this outcome?

4. What knowledge, skills, and identity would the person need to have in order to do these behaviors?

5. What supports and strategies might I offer and use to help this person toward the outcome?

6. What might I need, both internally and externally, to move this conversation forward?

These six questions form the basis for the box that follows. You don't need to "work the map" in a box or in any specific format, but it is on the facing page to give you a sense of how the map flows.

Chances are that you will have a good deal to consider as you work through the answers to these six questions with specific focus on a single, hard conversation. Typically, you can't state the answers in just a few sentences or with just a minute or two of reflection. Is it worth taking the time to engage in this process? Educators occasionally tell me that the assignment "isn't doable given the time crunch under which we work." I then ask them how long they have had the problem. And their typical response is several months. For some, even longer! From this, it should be evident that forming thoughtful responses to these questions is, indeed, a worthwhile use of your time. In the next section, I will drill down into each question, offering more nuance and substance so that you see how the process of thinking through this map can help you be more deliberate, empathic, and ultimately more productive.

DRILLING DOWN INTO THE SIX QUESTIONS: THE FIRST TWO QUESTIONS

1. What is the presenting problem?

2. What is the tentative outcome?

3. What are specific desired behaviors connected to this outcome?

4. What knowledge, skills, and identity would the person need to have in order to do these behaviors?

5. What supports and strategies might I offer and use to help this person toward the outcome?

6. What might I need, both internally and externally, to move this conversation forward?

Outcome Map

1. What is the problem?

2. What do you want to see instead (tentative outcome)?

3. What does it look like/sound like?

4. Why might the person not be doing the behaviors?

5. What supports might you offer?

6. What supports do you need?

—From *Having Hard Conversations*
by Jennifer Abrams (2009), p. 55

Questions 1 and 2: What is the presenting problem, and what do you want to see instead?

Getting down to what the real problem is can be tricky. When asked what the challenge truly is, many of us cannot articulate it. We hem and haw and circle around naming the exact problem. We can't find the words and then we get frustrated. We must take the time to discern and then articulate what we are bothered about, what we don't see happening, what isn't okay for students—and do so as precisely as we can. We owe it to those with whom we work to recognize how abstract our concerns can sound and to try our best to be as clear as we can be.

Can you describe the presenting problem in terms of the district's standards for this person's work? And, as we move from presenting problem to tentative outcome (from question 1 to 2), can you articulate what you want to see instead in a more proactive, future-focused way? Moving from *what is* to *what can be* frees both parties to look forward rather than dwelling on the present state of affairs.

Could you look at the following documents for specificity in articulating the problem?

- lesson plan templates offered by the school

- standards for teaching practice within the district

- specific English learner strategies that should be incorporated

- culturally proficient instructional designs that support all students

- clear instructions for what constitutes a satisfactory performance

- timelines and checklists for what needs to be done and when

Can you take neutral and professional words from already created documents and use them to state your concern? Professional and common language that is already in use in your district or organization is beyond helpful when trying to speak to a challenge you are facing. The wording is already known by both parties and it is neutral, which helps keep the tone professional.

Moving From Question 1 (Presenting Problem) to Question 2 (Tentative Outcome): Moving From Existing State to Desired State	
Existing State (Problem)	**Desired State (Outcome)**
Checks for understanding in classroom lesson were insufficient in number to assess student learning effectively	Need an increased number of checks for understanding during the lesson

Existing State (Problem)	Desired State (Outcome)
Teacher's use of sarcastic comments in class could be creating an unsafe environment for student learning	Teacher doesn't use sarcastic comments in class and instead uses supportive language to encourage student safety in the classroom environment
Team member is not demonstrating collaborative behaviors during team meetings	Collaborative behaviors (verbal and nonverbal) are used consistently during team meetings by team member

Watch Out for "Ouch" Language

When a principal in my training suggested he was going to speak to his assistant principal because she wasn't "leadership material," I referred to his proposed statement as "ouch" language. We worked on not only reframing and restating the concern in a professional manner, but also helping him to articulate specific, measurable behaviors that the assistant principal could enact to convey her leadership capacity to others and using the district's job expectations document as a place from which to get some specificity. Leaving others feeling personally belittled with statements that diminish their desire to improve is unhelpful and just plain wrong. Don't judge the person. Judge the behavior.

In our hard conversations, avoid slinging an "ouch" as your first move. We need to let go of the heat and the attitude, and name our concern in a professional and humane way. This doesn't mean your frustration isn't warranted nor your judgment correct. The key is to temper your language in how you communicate your concern.

Watch Your Adjectives!

Watch those judgmental adjectives (lazy, chaotic), generalizations (always, never), those qualifiers and modifiers in your presentation of the concern. Instead of saying, "You are an ineffective teacher who ignores your students' needs," you might instead speak to strategies that one can incorporate into one's lesson that meet students' needs for belonging and safety. Instead of saying, "You aren't productive. You waste time and are lazy," could you describe what a productive set of completed tasks might look like?

Drilling Down on Questions 1 and 2: Two Frames

The tasks of the job are so easy to describe. The objectives are on the whiteboard. Attendance is taken. The teacher arrives on time. The papers are graded. How simple it is to ascertain and point out objective evidence about these types of behaviors! Yet, we know our work is much more complicated than that. Intellectual, social, and emotional skill sets aren't as easy to describe. Articulating problems beyond specific skills and moving to the challenges of will or EQ, emotional intelligence, or psychological capabilities requires different language. Below are two frames through which to filter what you might want to say as you define the presenting problem.

Frame 1: States of Mind

Garmston and Costa in *Cognitive Coaching: Developing Self-Directed Leaders and Learners* (2015) describe five "states of mind" that may keep an individual from meeting an organizational, personal, or professional obligation.

Might the problem you are trying to articulate be *within* one of these five categories?

1. **Efficacy**—*Knowing that one has the capacity to make a difference and being willing and able to do so.* Perhaps the individual you are talking to does not feel resourceful or capable and as a result possibly blames others or shuts down?

Might the presenting problem be one about resourcefulness and taking responsibility and building the skills to do so?

2. **Flexibility**—*Knowing one has and can develop options to consider and being willing to acknowledge and demonstrate respect and empathy for diverse perspectives.* The individual doesn't see beyond his or her point of view and cannot yet see another's way of looking at the world.

Might the presenting problem be about a lack of respect for other people's points of view and the ways to demonstrate respect for other's perspectives?

3. **Craftsmanship**—*Seeking precision, refinement, and mastery. Striving for exactness of critical thought processes. Details matter.* Maybe the person is a big-picture thinker and the striving for accuracy and specifics isn't his or her forte. Yet accuracy is a key part of the work he or she needs to do.

Might the presenting problem be about precision and the ability to be more "micro" in one's focus and get down to the details?

4. **Consciousness**—*Monitoring one's own values, intentions, thoughts, and behaviors and their effects.* Perhaps the individual isn't aware of what she is doing or saying and its impact on others.

Might the presenting problem be about increasing awareness of one's impact?

5. **Interdependence**—*Being part of a team or larger group.* Perhaps the individual is not yet team savvy and doesn't recognize how to be a good group member, how to learn from a group, or how to "play well" with other adults in the school.

Might the *presenting problem* be about the need for an interdependent mindset and building a set of collaborative behaviors?

Frame 2: Emotional, Intellectual, and Psychological Capabilities

The second frame is grounded in the work of psychologist Robert Sternberg. Sternberg, in his book *Why Smart People Can Be So Stupid* (2002), speaks to several challenges people at work face beyond their intellectual capacity to do the tasks assigned to them. Being "smart" may not include the emotional capacities and self-regulation that are required to be effective in a given situation. Might the following characteristics help explain why some individuals are challenged and might they help you in crafting appropriate language for presenting the problem? Remember that the word *lack* can be a trigger for many people, so framing the tentative outcome without this word will most likely result in a more productive framing of the outcome.

1. **Lack of impulse control**—Habitual impulsiveness gets in the way of optimal performance. Some go with the first solution that pops into their heads.

2. **Lack of perseverance and perseveration**—Some people give up too easily, while others are unable to stop even when the quest will clearly be fruitless.

3. **Using the wrong abilities**—People may not be using the right abilities for the tasks in which they are engaged.

4. **Inability to translate thought into action**—Some people seem buried in thought. They have good ideas but rarely seem able to do anything about them.

5. **Lack of product orientation**—Some people seem more concerned about the process than the result of activity.

6. **Inability to complete tasks**—For some people, nothing ever draws to a close. Perhaps it's fear of what they would do next or fear of becoming hopelessly enmeshed in detail.

7. **Failure to initiate**—Still others are unwilling or unable to initiate a project. It may be indecision or fear of commitment.

8. **Procrastination**—Some people are unable to act without pressure. They may also look for little things to do in order to put off the big ones.

9. **Misattribution of blame**—Some people always blame themselves for even the slightest mishap. Some always blame others.

10. **Excessive dependency**—Some people expect others to do for them what they ought to be doing themselves.

11. **Distractibility and lack of concentration**—Even some very intelligent people have very short attention spans.

12. **Spreading oneself too thin or too thick**—Undertaking too many activities may result in none being completed on time. Undertaking too few can also result in missed opportunities and reduced levels of accomplishment.

13. **Inability to delay gratification**—Some people reward themselves and are rewarded by others for finishing small tasks, while avoiding bigger tasks that would earn them larger rewards.

14. **Inability to see the forest for the trees**—Some people become obsessed with details and are either unwilling or unable to see or deal with the larger picture in the projects they undertake.

15. **Lack of balance between critical, analytical thinking and creative, synthetic thinking**—It is important for people to learn what kind of thinking is expected of them in each situation.

It might be difficult to directly lift one of these capabilities from the book and cite them in an actual conversation as connected to a job description or a union contract, but I imagine for some the language isn't too far off from the wording in district documents. As you consider the look-for behaviors in the next section—the specific actions you would like to see taken—you might understand more compassionately what stands between the individual and the action.

MOVING ON: QUESTION 3

1. What is the presenting problem?

2. What is the tentative outcome?

3. **What are specific desired behaviors connected to this outcome?**

4. What knowledge, skills, and identity would the person need to have in order to do these behaviors?

5. What supports and strategies might I offer and use to help this person toward the outcome?

6. What might I need, both internally and externally, to move this conversation forward?

We spend a lot of time with students describing what abstract ideas look like in practice. *Getting ready* for class means

- putting away your backpack

- getting notebook paper and a pen out

- putting yourself in your chair

- facing forward with eyes on the teacher

- putting your hands in your lap

- not speaking but keeping mouth shut

As we know with students, there are a lot of pieces to the getting-ready concept, and we wouldn't expect young people to understand all those behaviors without being very clear as to what they all are.

We have a tendency to think that adults, however, can just discern all the moving parts from one fuzzy concept and it isn't true or fair to expect that discernment all the time and from all people. We do need to be clearer around our concepts.

We certainly aren't trying to be patronizing, and we can avoid this perception by establishing the right tone. But it is essential that discrete explanations come into play. We cannot presume a common understanding when there isn't any. We cannot just codify one of the following and assume it is understood in the form of discrete, actionable behaviors.

For example, what do these concepts mean in action? The concepts below are followed by actions to show the difference between possibly fuzzy concept words and descriptors of behaviors. This isn't an exhaustive list, but you see differences between concept and action more clearly.

- **Engage students?** (put them into a cooperative learning activity, have students debate, do a lab experiment)

- **Be prepared?** (arrive in class at 7:30 a.m., have copies made, objective on board)

- **Incorporate technology?** (students use laptops, use document camera, seek out resources on the Web)

- **Be productive?** (complete tasks by end of work day, follow up on calls to parents, finish paperwork for other team members by deadline)

- **Take initiative?** (send e-mails to the team suggesting next steps, offer to take on a project, seek out a resource)

- **Be a team player?** (nod, offer validation, agree to your part of the planning, send follow-up e-mails)

- **Be a leader?** (be the facilitator at the meeting, agree to be on a subcommittee, be willing to work on a draft of a proposal, commit to attending a weekend workshop with a team)

- **Be a professional?** (participate in staff meetings without texting, greet others in the hallway, not sending reply-all e-mails unless warranted)

- **Be more positive?** (send a thank-you, sit at the table at the meeting and not far away, put elbows on the table and engage, nod and affirm verbally)

- **Be less negative?** (no eye rolling or sighing, being cautious with comments like "Why do we have to do this?," being mindful of tone and volume)

- **Care more?** (kneel down at student's level, fist bump, celebrate a birthday, welcome a student back after absence)

None of these concepts in and of themselves are wrong as stated and they are often used as presenting problems and tentative outcomes. But they may not be sufficient to communicate desired outcomes, behaviors, or actions. Giving specifics will get you further, and they are essential to planning a hard conversation that is skillful and compassionate. When someone asks you, "What exactly would that look like?" you have to be ready to describe the actions that demonstrate that concept.

"We're overwhelmed." "So am I."

Secretaries in one human resources office rallied together to get some relief from their bosses due to their hectic schedules. They set up a meeting and went in together as one unified front. Two administrators from HR were in the room, yellow pads and pens in hand. One secretary spoke for the group: "We are overwhelmed," she said. The assistant superintendent looked at her and said, "Me too. What would you like me to do about it?" The secretaries didn't have an answer. They expected their supervisor to have the answer. Because the secretaries had never moved beyond voicing the complaint to articulating their desired solutions, they walked out of the room without their requests being met. Specifics matter.

Being Too Fuzzy: Common Core Standards Implementation and the Kennedy Moon Launch

I spent time with a group of administrators at their start of school retreat. I came in as the superintendent was giving a pep talk about implementation of Common Core standards. He stated that, "just like John Kennedy's vision for a space program and the eventual moon launch that Kennedy never had the chance to see, we too are 'going to the moon.' Kennedy didn't know how, but he had faith and a vision. And just as the district might not know how we are going to get there with Common Core standards implementation, with faith we will get there." Not many school administrators were impressed by the superintendent's speech. More details might have given some comfort, security, and direction to the group of principals needing to lead the way and to see the implementation the standards back at their sites. "Kennedy did it and we can too" wasn't enough. Detailed implementation plans with specific supports provided from the district office would have been appreciated.

Have a set of specific behaviors at the ready if the person says, "What exactly do you mean?"—visible, audible, actual behaviors. It will move your planning further into a reality than broad concepts.

NEXT UP: QUESTION 4

1. What is the presenting problem?

2. What is the tentative outcome?

3. What are specific desired behaviors connected to this outcome?

4. **What knowledge, skills, and identity would the person need to have in order to do these behaviors?**

5. What supports and strategies might I offer and use to help this person toward the outcome?

6. What might I need, both internally and externally, to move this conversation forward?

What knowledge, skills, and identity will the person need to have in order to achieve the desired outcomes you just mentioned? We are about to have a hard conversation with this individual, and it is only fair to ask what this person would need to know and be able to do in order to do the task set before them. In terms of knowledge and skills, sometimes the person honestly didn't get the memo, have the knowledge, take the course, or understand the directions. Maybe they don't know how to work the computer, use the document camera, fill out the paperwork online, add formative assessment techniques to the lesson, or cue students to attention. So we need to know the person has that knowledge or those skills. These two parts of the question are somewhat easy to answer if you know the individual. And if they don't have the knowledge or skills, it is somewhat easy to provide the support to get that information to the person.

In this book, I hope to provide a more nuanced approach to this question: What can we know about the other person that can help us become more sensitive to their perspective? The *identity* part of the question asks us to be flexible and see things from the other person's perspective. You may approach the problem with the thought, "This is a professional exchange. How much do I really need to know about the person? We hired them. They should do their job." In fact, knowing more about your colleague than their job title is essential to the success of the conversation. No one leaves their whole identity at the door when they walk into work. Being aware of who you work with is so important in having a humane conversation. I will provide several filters and ways of looking at this question on the following pages. I call it moving from egocentric to allocentric. Follow me.

Moving From Egocentric to Allocentric: Looking Through Our Filters of Perception

One of the moments in the thinking before we speak that can be most powerful is when we go from egocentric to allocentric—from self-focused to other-focused. Allocentric means centering your interest and attention on another person. Being humane in this context means being in touch with how the person at the receiving end of the hard conversation experiences the exchange in the moment, beginning with an appreciation of the filters of perception.

Possible Filters of Perception (Not an Exhaustive List)

- Social-emotional or cognitive
- Past experiences and current reality
- Personal and family challenges
- Mental health challenges
- Learning challenges
- Personal and professional attachments
- Generational
- Race, culture, or country of origin
- Class
- Gender
- Beliefs/values and mindsets

Filters of perception are the lenses through which we examine the world. Examples include our race, class, gender, and country of origin. How might these lenses affect our behavior? How might they limit or give us permission to take action? Could they bias us toward or against certain actions? Other examples of filters to consider are regional affiliation, religion, family status, and educational level.

Considering where the other person is "coming from" and where you are coming from *might* give you insight into what might be stopping the person at the present moment from enacting the desired behavior that you are having the hard conversation about to begin with. Being aware of the other person's filters—as well as our own—is a start to seeing what might be stopping the other person from doing the behaviors as stated in our expectations and seeing what our biases and expectations are from a new point of view. Think about yourself and the other person and all the filters you bring to your work. It's the "deeper dive" we often don't have time to take. The filters addressed here are not all filters that impact one's perspective, nor should you take yourself through all of them too intently and overwhelm yourself to the point that you can't see the forest for the trees. But knowing these filters are ever-present and impact one's work makes taking an allocentric perspective all the more important.

Filter 1: Emotional or Cognitive Filters

Most every challenge faced has its cognitive and emotional components. We think professional expectations are most often logical and rational in nature. Fill out the paperwork, come to work on time, complete a task. But oftentimes there is so much more to things than meets the eye.

Example: While it may seem like a given that principals write evaluations and have deadlines for submitting them, some principals may have bad memories of writing assignments from their high school English classes. Perhaps they don't feel competent as writers. Such confidence gaps can impact the work of writing evaluations many years after high school graduation. Even if the task you are requesting to be completed is as basic as learning to use a new computer application or any number of "mechanical" changes, ask yourself what else might be happening. Might negative emotions stemming from past experiences be blocking success in the present?

Filter 2: Filters of Past Experience Compared to Current Experience

Although many of us assume that policies and practices are similar from school to school and district to district, this may not always be the case. Despite the presence of structural similarities such as classrooms and schedules, there is so much that differs school to school based on culture, grade level, and climate. Expectations three miles up the road are different than at the school three miles down, even if they are in the same "unified" school district. Sometimes we need to reclarify what is expected at "our" workplace.

What might this person *think* is okay when it isn't okay here? What might the school need to enforce, value, acknowledge, or give permission to in order to help this person do the actions requested?

Example: The new teacher assumed that writing disciplinary referrals was the norm in her new school. She had come from a school that valued such a response from teachers when things went wrong and a trip to the assistant principal if even more went wrong. In her first semester she wrote several referrals. Unfortunately, it was an incorrect assumption to assume that was the norm in her new building. She soon got labeled as a "difficult" teacher. A frank discussion regarding the differences between the *other* school and *this* school would have helped her adjust more successfully. Yet no one thought to acknowledge where she'd been and how significantly different the new school was. Instead, her colleagues assumed that she was as an authoritarian figure—a judgment that caused a few bumps in the road for her first few years.

Filter 3: Filters of Personal Challenges or Learning Challenges

These filters ask us to recognize what is going on for the individual and to care for them while holding on to having them accountable for their professional work. Some questions to consider in the context of care and accountability include the following:

- Do you know if there are any personal challenges currently taking place in this person's life? (Some examples are listed in the text box below.)

- If so, is there a support or an accommodation you can provide for now?

Personal Challenges
• Being the caretaker of a sick child/parent/spouse/partner • Being a new parent/stepparent • Other big life events—graduations, moves • Divorce • Death/grief • Financial troubles • Physical illnesses • Depression • Anxiety • Alcoholism/drug addiction • Anger issues • Eating disorders • Traumatic events

Other challenges may stem from cognitive or learning differences, such as those in the next text box. They are quite different than the challenges named above, but they too are often deemed personal and can be hidden from others in the workplace. We as educators can work with an understanding of situational challenges, or with learning needs if we know about them. We can modify and accommodate. And, while we show care to our colleague we need to hold them accountable for the work they do on behalf of our students and the school.

Cognitive and/or Learning Differences

- Executive functioning/organizational skills/memory issues
- ADD/ADHD
- Impulse control
- Autism spectrum/social pragmatics challenges
- Visual/auditory processing problems
- Dyslexia

Whether the challenges are personal or rooted in individual differences, part of maintaining the right balance between care and accountability is having a knowledge of appropriate supports within your building or district. There is a text box below that mentions supports most districts provide.

Supports You Can Access

Do you know the support systems that are in place for employees at your district? Are there folks who can be "thought partners" with you as you think through what next steps might be? Are there colleagues who can send you to the right person to give you a legal, psychological, or medical perspective if you need one?

- Human resources personnel
- Employee assistance program personnel
- Psychologists/social workers
- Speech-language pathologists
- Professional development specialists

Filter 4: Personal and Professional Attachments

With whom is the other person affiliated? Who do they admire or respect? Chances are that this person (the *influencer*) has the potential to have an impact on the outcomes of the hard conversation.

Does what I am going to say ring true with the beliefs and assumptions of the influencer? How might the influencer impact the follow-through (or lack thereof) after the conversation? What can I do or say, if anything, to acknowledge this? This person could be a union member, a strong informal mentor, one of the team-level or departmental colleagues, a spouse, or partner. If this influencer has the ear of the person in need of the hard conversation, can you anticipate what they might say?

Filter 5: Generational Filter

In the book *The Multigenerational Workplace: Communicate, Collaborate, & Create Community*, Valerie von Frank and I (Abrams & von Frank, 2013) mention sticking points—places where different generations have different ways of working. While there is *no* one right way, there might be a generational lens through which your colleague is looking and hence, he or she doesn't see the work in the same way you do. I encourage schools to be generationally sensitive and flexible *and* speak with strong sense of school values.

How do we expect others to behave in terms of the following:

- Speaking about the work they do in the school and speaking about our students

- Speaking to other adults in the school, including expectations of tone and language

- Honoring policies, deadlines, and procedures. (First, determine if there is transparency around the rationale for these protocols and an understanding of what happens when some don't follow them.)

- What is our sense of the individual versus collective balancing act? What needs to be done in a group? What can be done solo?

Hard conversations often take place without the mindfulness of the generational differences at play. Isn't *everyone* like this?

One new administrator called me to come to his beginning of the year meeting as he realized that half his school had been hired in the last three years. The rest had been there for quite a while. Better than having hard conversations from the get-go is to have everyone be very clear about school norms and expectations regardless of age or years of experience. This filter is at play more times than you know.

Is Your Hard Conversation About One of These Issues? Could Be a Generational Difference at Play . . .

The Delineators	Boomers	Xers	Millennials
Perspective on work	Your work isn't just your work but a calling.	You want a life-work balance and see work in a bigger scheme of life.	There will be many careers so I might want to move on sooner than others think I should.
Communication style	Everyone deserves someone to be kind and a bit tentative during a hard conversation. It will go more smoothly.	When others are beating around the bush, I find myself growing frustrated. Just tell me what you think.	I have lived with feedback and expectations since elementary school. Please continue to tell me what is expected. Be clear about it upfront.

(Continued)

(Continued)

The Delineators	Boomers	Xers	Millennials
Response to policies and procedures	Don't people understand we have policies for a reason? Why do they need to be so resistant to them? Policies help us with the work.	Does every little policy have a purpose? They seem to be obstructing the work. If you want us to follow them, be transparent with their rationales.	I have been given rubrics and checklists since I was in elementary school. I am happy to follow them, but please be clear about all policies upfront. I don't like to be caught unaware when I have done something "wrong" but it was never stated.
Focus on work projects	Relationships matter and results do too. But relationships are *really* important. Process is key.	Just tell me what the task is and I will finish it. I can do it solo and don't need a team around me to do so.	Been in teams since elementary school. Very used to working in teams. Like them. We can do things asynchronously or in the same room. It's all good.
To what do I owe the next job?	Experience matters. Several years in a position gives me wisdom and insight that will help me in the next role.	Merit matters. If I do the roles in a shorter amount of time than my Boomer colleagues, but do a good job and interview well, years in the previous role shouldn't matter.	It is assumed there will be a next job. I want to be promoted and try new things. I was told I could do so much, so let's begin!

Filter 6: Culture, Race, or Country of Origin Filter

We have our filters—sometimes we just think that the view we have is the "correct view" without taking into consideration how that view is tinted by our background. There is a good chance that we *do* see things differently than others in so many ways. Am I using a cultural/race and/or country of origin lens to examine the challenge I am facing and if so, how does that impact the way I engage in the hard conversation?

In the book *Clash!: How to Thrive in a Multicultural World*, Markus and Conner (2014) speak to eight conflicts in the United States that could very well impact our work and our hard conversations. Might one of these lenses be impacting your hard conversation? Are you and your colleague the same or different in terms of the following identities, and how might your different perspectives be at play in this conflict?

1. White versus people of color

2. Men versus women

3. Rich versus poor

4. Religious liberals versus religious conservatives

5. East versus west (western versus eastern hemispheres)

6. Coasts versus heartland

7. Businesses versus nonprofits and governments

8. Global North versus Global South

Singleton and Linton (2006) speak about meaningful dialogue about race and discuss patterns of conversation across cultures as "White Talk and Color Commentary." White talk is more "verbal, impersonal, intellectual, and task oriented," while color commentary is more "nonverbal, personal, emotional, and process oriented" (p. 200). They caution that these trends may not be universal across all people of one race or another, but that these are common patterns of dialogue. I too have seen this pattern in conversation and believe it should be considered in the context of filters of perception and how our cultural lens impacts the content and the language patterns we use during conversation.

Country of Origin Stories Filter

Depending on your country of origin, there are different ways of communicating. Directly or indirectly? Immediately or after a while? With a great deal of focus on the task or more on the relationship? Different cultures have different values. Your hard conversation comes from your perspective on the world. Some examples:

One gentleman from rural Ireland, when asked how to start a hard conversation, said, "Bring them a coffee and have a sit." This might work for some but for others it could be too informal. It all depends on context.

In Jewish day schools there most always is a need for understanding the different communication patterns of Israelis and Americans and how those patterns could impact collaboration.

While working in Toronto (the most ethnically diverse city in North America) with instructional aides, not one person at the table was born in the country of Canada. Views of leading, deciding, disagreeing, scheduling, and communicating need to be understood in a global context.

For more information on this filter, read *The Culture Map: Breaking Through the Invisible Boundaries of Global Business* by Erin Meyer (2014).

> ## Class Filter
>
> Many (but not all) of the teachers and educators working in schools in the United States today are middle class. We work with students and some colleagues who come from a variety of socioeconomic backgrounds. How others view conflict and look at the decision making that would solve it might look different depending on one's socioeconomic status, upbringing, and individual circumstances, Typically, our white, middle-class citizenry has benefitted from our nation's schools in ways that may not apply to the less privileged. Be mindful that your way isn't the only way to be successful and that in other contexts we wouldn't be nearly as fortunate.

Filter 7: Gender Filter

Katty Kay and Claire Shipman wrote an article titled "The Confidence Gap," which appeared in the May 2014 issue of *The Atlantic*. In the article, they wrote,

> There is a particular crisis for women—a vast confidence gap that sepa-rates the sexes. Compared with men, women don't consider themselves as ready for promotions, they predict they'll do worse on tests, and they generally underestimate their abilities.

The idea of "the confidence gap" is spot-on in so many interactions I have seen with female educators at all levels. I have become accustomed to state-ments like the following: "How does he get away with that? When he says it, it is viewed as assertive, but if I ever said it I'd be called a drama queen."

In hard conversations, regardless of gender, ask yourself, "Is this something that is educationally sound, physically unsafe, or emotionally damaging to oth-ers?" If so, you need to speak up on behalf of others with confidence in knowing that you aren't being too touchy-feely or overly sensitive.

Men often feel more comfortable speaking in whole groups than women and consider themselves worthy of more airtime. They also don't hesitate to claim this airtime. If there are norms for group interaction that include assumptions about airtime, they should be treated as public agreement. Again, a disclaimer: these observations aren't meant to apply to *all* men or women. At the same time, I encourage readers to be mindful that this gender filter might be at play in a hard conversation.

Filter 8: Filter of Beliefs/Mindsets/Values

Another dimension at play in why someone might not be doing the behav-iors you and your district ask of him or her could be a difference in beliefs as to the purpose of schools or how organizations should be managed.

We don't get much of a chance to dig under the surface to truly consider what our philosophies are around why we act as we do until it gets ugly. Do we act under the assumption that intelligence is "fixed" and some kids are just des-tined to drop out? Or, do we believe our job is to foster growth, regardless of where our students start out? Do we think it is our job to do (fill in the blank)? Lift off the surface soil and there are deep values at play. These deeply held beliefs should be discussed more openly at all times during the year, rather than waiting for a hard conversation. Ask yourself:

- What are the key assumptions and beliefs about work and schools that is underlying my hard conversation?

- Do we know what the person's key assumptions and beliefs are around school, teaching, students, families, and work?

- Do we have the ability to articulate those beliefs and mindsets and practice challenging others and themselves around strongly held beliefs?

Maybe your hard conversation is being enacted because you care about some virtues and issues more than others, and you don't see the other person sharing these values.

Do you value students learning how to follow specific traditions or to think beyond one's group? Do you want to spend your class time teaching content or social-emotional learning? Nothing is an either–or. A strong belief that we should follow certain foundational ways of interacting with rules and others might not have been articulated but could be at play in the hard conversation you wish to have.

Differences in Belief Systems

A person's ideologies significantly influence their educational decisions. . . . . recognize colleagues' prevailing educational ideologies through their use of metaphors, educational goals, instructional methods, approaches to assessing outcomes, and teaching.

—From *Cognitive Coaching* (2nd ed.), Arthur Costa and Robert Garmston (2002), p. 256

Think about what you believe education is designed to do and how that might differ with others on your staff. Might surfacing your beliefs be a part of uncovering the challenges you face? Maybe you believe in school as a place to transmit basic knowledge, skills, and traditions, and your colleague believes school is to nurture the child's creativity and full development. Belief systems about the purpose of school are always at play.

Schwartz's 10 Values: How Do They Connect With Your Hard Conversation?

Professor Shalom Schwartz (2006) from Hebrew University in Israel studied values across many cultures and has spoken of these 10 researched values as "desirable, trans-situational goals, varying in importance that serve as guiding principles in people's lives" (p. 1). Schwartz says they vary in importance depending on who you are, where you live and work, what you value. Hard conversations, at their foundation, *might* happen because what you value isn't what the other person values and it is causing a "rub" in the work that is taking place at the school.

For many educators the following five values are most important to them. Again, it isn't all educators but given the system in many of the schools today, we live out these values in our rules, disciplinary actions, schedules, celebrations, curriculum choices, and so on.

(Continued)

(Continued)

- **Benevolence**—making sure those with whom you have frequent contact are taken care of; caring about other's well-being
- **Tradition**—respect for the customs and ideas that your community holds
- **Conformity**—a desire to not violate social expectations or norms and instead behave in a way that the collective feels is appropriate
- **Security**—safety in relationships with others and with self
- **Universalism**—understanding, appreciation, tolerance, and protection for the welfare of all people

Oftentimes, we have a hard conversation with someone when we feel these values are not recognized or are simply tossed aside for other values.

And, when values deemed more important by an individual are those mentioned below, we might also speak up.

- **Power**—social status and control or dominance over people and resources
- **Achievement**—personal success according to social standards—note the word, *personal*—we value achievement and success of students but we don't always like if our colleague wants to "stand out" for something—it creates a "tall poppy" situation and the group isn't pleased
- **Hedonism**—pleasure or sensuous gratification for oneself—not why we got into the business of teaching—to be self-absorbed and focus on our needs
- **Stimulation**—excitement, novelty, and challenge
- **Self-Direction**—independent thought and action; choosing, creating, exploring

Our views on what students should learn—self-directedness or rules, social-emotional learning or academic content—is aligned with our mindsets and our values. How should we discipline students? What should we emphasize in our teaching? Should we have class rankings? Is service learning a component of what should be taught? When you think about what you value and what you feel school should be about, you might find yourself in a values clarification exercise you never meant to be in and that is when a hard conversation might take place.

Ask yourself the following:

- Might my values be different than those of my colleagues?
- Am I more interested in self-direction and stimulation while my colleague is more interested in tradition and conformity?
- Might we figure out how to acknowledge these values and possibly meet in the middle?

Viewing the scenario "from the balcony" with the awareness that that our values and mindsets transcend this specific conversation and are often at the center of big challenges that countries face, takes us out of our personalizing of the conflict into a bigger and generally more valuable discussion.

COMING BACK TO THE OUTCOME MAP QUESTIONS: THE FINAL TWO QUESTIONS, 5 AND 6

1. What is the presenting problem?

2. What is the tentative outcome?

3. What are specific desired behaviors connected to this outcome?

4. What knowledge, skills, and identity would the person need to have in order to do these behaviors?

5. **What supports and strategies might I offer and use to help this person toward the outcome?**

6. **What might I need, both internally and externally, to move this conversation forward?**

The last two questions in the Outcome Map complete our prethinking before we move to scripting our initial words. We have gone through our specific actions that we would like to see and all the thinking around why the person might or might not be doing these behaviors at this point. Now we are coming back to ourselves. We are moving back to what we can do with this information we gathered to support the individual in case he or she says, "What are you going to do to help me with this?" It is a humane, growth-producing act to think through questions 5 and 6 before we speak up.

Question 5: What supports and strategies might I offer and use to help this person toward the outcome?

Now that you have looked at the problem humanely, through a variety of filters, you are better able to answer the question, "What supports might I offer?" Supports are offered when the individual asks for help on following through with whatever change you have requested in the hard conversation, if they need some from you at all. And, after the prethinking you have done whatever support you can offer might align more with the specific person and his or her needs. They are more customized and personal. And when you say, "Would this be helpful?," it comes from a place of greater awareness and empathy.

Supports and strategies to assist the individual could include but are not limited to:

- Coaching, mentoring, a colleague's help in moving to the next step

- Providing resources, materials, access to links on the Web

- Offering training opportunities

- Doing modeling of the skill in the classroom

- Providing time to do the work outside of school

- Providing assistance in planning

- Videotaping

- Creating checklists, templates

You cannot presume that the person has the bandwidth to think through what he or she might need in order to execute the behaviors. "They can figure it out from here," might be true and might not be true. A few suggestions are helpful to start the ball rolling. Offering ideas and supports shows that you are in a growth-producing space and not a "gotcha" frame of mind.

Question 6: What might I need, both internally and externally, to move this conversation forward?

The final question in the map asks us to consider what *we* might need in order to move forward in a growth-producing way. Many individuals in my workshops say this is the question they *never* ask. They get so involved in the other person and supporting the other person that they forget this conversation also includes looking at their supports and they might need in order to have a hard conversation that will have the greatest chance to move the ball forward. Question 6 asks two things:

1. What do I need to do *internally* to be in a good place emotionally in order to have this hard conversation?

   Meditation, quiet time?

   A good night's sleep?

   A good breakfast?

   Listening to some great music in the car on the way to work?

   Making sure I get to work out so I am less anxious and agitated?

   Being well hydrated or caffeinated?

2. What do I need to do *externally* to be at a good place to have this conversation?

   Do I need to have a preliminary discussion with my HR department to be certain that my proposed hard conversation is in alignment with the contract?

   Do I need another person to be in the room with me?

   Do I need a set of bullet points of the "look fors" and the supports to offer on a piece of paper so I don't go off track?

   Do I need to have determined a location to have the conversation? A desk or a couch or a round table? Have it in their classroom, or if I have an office do we speak in my office?

Do I need the printed-out job description with me?

Do I need to have the door open or shut for the most humane, productive discussion?

Do I need a timer, or do I need this to take as much time as needed?

There are so many factors at play in our conversations—so many lenses we don't have time to truly acknowledge or aspects that we are unaware of. And honestly, we don't take enough time to clarify our own values that should be acknowledged, articulated, and asserted. Thinking about these six questions is critical for us as we become more humane and growth-inspiring professionals.

THE CONVERSATION CONTINUES . . .

Clash! How to Survive in a Multicultural World by Hazel Rose Markus and Alana Conner, Plume, 2014

"Coaching the Toxic Leader" by Manfred F. R. Kets de Vries, *Harvard Business Review,* April 2014; https://hbr.org/2014/04/coaching-the-toxic-leader/ar/1

"The Confidence Gap" by Katty Kay and Claire Shipman, *The Atlantic,* May 2014

Courageous Conversations About Race: A Field Guide for Achieving Equity in Schools by Glenn E. Singleton and Curtis Linton, Corwin, 2006

Cognitive Coaching: Developing Self-Directed Leaders and Learners (3rd ed.) by Arthur Costa and Robert Garmston with Jane Ellison and Carolee Hayes, Rowman & Littlefield, 2015

Crucial Accountability: Tools for Resolving Violated Expectations, Broken Commitments and Bad Behavior by Kerry Patterson, Joseph Grenny, David Maxfield, Ron McMillan, and Al Switzler, VitalSmarts, 2013

The Culture Map: Breaking Through the Invisible Boundaries of Global Business by Erin Meyer, Public Affairs, 2014

The Multigenerational Workplace: Communicate, Collaborate, & Create Community by Jennifer Abrams and Valerie von Frank, Corwin, 2013

The Righteous Mind: Why Good People Are Divided by Politics and Religion by Jonathan Haidt, Vintage, 2013

Why Smart People Can Be So Stupid by R. J. Sternberg, Oxford University Press, 2002; www.yourmorals.org

Organizational Politics, Working With Supervisors or Groups, and Hard Conversations

4

Men cannot see their reflections in running water, but only in still water.

—Chuang-Tzu

Chapter 3 focused on *the other*—*one* other person. However, it isn't always just one person that we need to pay attention to as we frame our hard conversation. We might need to take a look at the organization in which we work. Understandably, we want to have one hard conversation and be done. Yet, the challenge is at times bigger than just one person. It goes beyond one person; it is an organizational challenge that has happened before, with many other people, for a long time. Sometimes the challenge you are facing is enmeshed into the culture of the organization, and if we are honest with ourselves one hard conversation will not change behavior on a bigger scale. This chapter discusses hard conversations that need to happen when the conversation is with a group or across a district and when the hard conversations need to happen "up"—hard conversations with your supervisor. Both types can be tricky but are necessary if you want to support the organization in moving forward.

ORGANIZATIONAL CHANGE AND HARD CONVERSATIONS

We see these conversations at play every year in schools. Here are a few examples of those tricky group challenges at the organizational level.

- Common assessments now expected *across* a grade level and/or *throughout* a content area and some are not on board

- Alignment with Common Core State Standards *across* departments and some are still working the "old way"

- Changes in job descriptions and titles at district level in a *"re-org"* in order to create a more efficient district office administration and there is a possibility of an undercurrent of hurt and anger

- The *whole* of middle school is moving going toward a Humanities 6-7-8 teaching of the curriculum instead of one English class and a separate social studies class, each taught by a different teacher and they don't necessarily respect each other

- Deciding that push in versus pull out is better for inclusion of students with special needs and thus co-teaching is now the norm, scheduling *of two* teachers in *one* classroom and the general studies teachers don't get along with the special education teachers and both groups are now co-teaching together "for the sake of the students." It isn't going well across the board.

- Absorbing a pilot program within a stable department and *changing up all the personnel* and their titles. Drama could ensue.

In instances like these, thinking strategically about how to have a hard conversation with the right people, not person, is essential. It requires a systems thinking mindset and a sense of organizational and political savvy.

When things get this big in scope and it appears in the rollout that those in charge of implementation are confused about what's next, irritation and resistance become common. Have those who are in charge been empathic and strategic? If not, one might need to have a hard conversation "up" to address concerns. Organizational challenges take systems-savvy thinking and planning.

Parking Lot Organizational Savvy Etiquette: A Cautionary Tale

A department chair called me to process a hard conversation in which she had been the recipient. The week before she had seen the superintendent in her school parking lot and, as an open person known for her candidness, she had expressed some concerns to him before walking to her classroom. A few days later she was asked to the principal's office

> where the principal expressed her displeasure at hearing about the inter-action. "Everyone is so 'touchy,'" she commented to me. As we looked at the politics at play in the interactions, she saw the system at play. Her complaints were heard by the superintendent who went back to share them with the assistant superintendent, who brought them to the atten-tion of the principal, who was surprised at how a teacher at her site had gone "above her" and talked not to *her* boss, but her *boss's boss*! For someone who isn't thinking about hierarchy, this overstepping of bound-aries didn't even cross the department chair's mind. The organizational ideas of power, authority, hierarchy, and protocol weren't even on her radar. Good lesson in being systems savvy.

A question to ask yourself:

WHAT ARE THE POLITICS "IN PLAY" THAT I NEED TO ACKNOWLEDGE AS I MOVE FORWARD?

Hard conversations don't happen in a vacuum. They happen within a system of relationships. Teachers, busy working with students, don't always have the mindset to think about the politics at play in the current system as much as they should. They're busy focusing on the students. It's understandable. And yet, if you want to make systems change as a teacher leader or administrator, it's critical to be aware of what is going on from the "balcony point of view." There are explicit *and implicit* norms at play all the time.

There are organizational assumptions and processes at work. All of us need to understand what *isn't* being said as much as what is, because it impacts our ability to be influential.

Some educators tell me they "aren't political." They don't want to get involved in the "drama" of the organization. They went into teaching to avoid all that organizational "stuff"—all the ego, the fear, the unspoken ten-sion, and anxiety. Yet when someone is released from their position, there are tears and snipes and bcc'd e-mails. But as Steve Maraboli (n.d.), behavioral science academic, once said, "Your fear of the truth does not hide or dilute it." We have come to terms with the reality that we are working within a system and we need to know how to communicate well within that system.

A key question that brings you to the "organizational balcony" is "What is the ripple effect of the hard conversation on the other folks in the department or school or district?" If one wants to roll out a new initiative, might you realize that not only will the teachers in that department be affected but all instructional aides too, so here comes the special education department. Then someone is married to some-one in your department and so she shares the news with her departmental col-leagues and rumors spread. Then the schedule needs to be changed, which brings in a whole new slew of folks who are impacted and then more drama ensues. "*They* always get what *they* want." "*We always* have to deal with their changes." You see how it goes—an organizational rollout gone awry. We've all been there.

UNDERSTANDING ORGANIZATIONAL POLITICS AND THE INTERESTS OF OTHERS

One of my cognitive crushes is on Dr. Robert Marshak. Marshak, author of *Covert Processes at Work: Managing the Five Hidden Dimensions of Organizational Change,* opened my eyes to seeing through, not just the allocentric lens, but the organizational lens. Marshak (2006) has a set of questions to think about in terms of organizational change. Ask yourself the following questions as you look toward the success of your organizational hard conversation and the implementation of new behaviors you wish to see.

- **Who are the stakeholders with interests related to the change, and based on their needs how might they perceive this change?** There is always someone affected by the conversation even though they aren't there—team members, secretaries, colleagues, family members. Is what you are asking going to impact others and how so? Be prepared to consider shifts in these lives as well and how you could support those individuals too. For example, will a secretary be given additional work if there is a re-org and her boss is promoted? If so, will she be given a raise?

- **What sources of power or influence do these stakeholders have to impact the change?** Do they have greater "pull" than you? Will they get in your way? Consider their resistance and how it could affect you. For example, if you do something in educational services, how does that impact human resources? How long have those individuals been in the district? Might you need to go rally their support if you are new and they are the "old guard" and might want things to stay status quo?

- **How will you deal with each critical stakeholder to ensure support for the change?** How might you anticipate what these individuals will be thinking and speak to it during your conversation? Perhaps address their concerns from the start? How can you get ahead of the resistance and manage the response? These other people might not champion your outcome but at least they won't deliberately resist. For example, going to informal, perhaps not positional, power players and getting their "take" on a change so they were in the know from the beginning might assure you won't be rolled over on during a major meeting.

- **Will you need to modify your proposal to gain enough support by those who could block your plan?** Are you willing to modify what you want if someone outside the conversation holds more sway than you and, if so, how? It is best if you have a few ideas before the conversation as to what your negotiables and non-negotiables are. I watched a block schedule roll-out go through many iterations in order to not be totally opposed and revolted against.

- **How will we continue to monitor the shifting needs, interests, and political processes as the change unfolds?** Remember, these hard conversations are not one-time "talks"—these hard conversations are ongoing processes that will take *several* discussions and most likely several months; if we look at research on change, it could take years. Things will shift that you need to be aware of and be ready for. It is a marathon, not a sprint. Every interaction counts. Every hello in the hallway. Every exchange is another opportunity to see what the needs are at this time.

Remember, the Rational Isn't Always What Is at Play

A school district is doing a reorganization of their district office roles and responsibilities. The boxes are labeled on the sheet; the staff has been notified. The roles have been dispersed. Changes have been made. Additional personnel have been included. Some are getting new titles. Others are being promoted. But the boxes on the chart are *just the beginning.* If this hard conversation is done with respect and with forethought, the resistance, shock, and dismay will be lessened—but *not* eliminated. Every group hard conversation is a bumpy ride, but some are made bumpier by *not* taking into consideration the organizational covert dynamics of loss, jealousy, and power. Every conversation on the table has one that is happening *under the table.* Think Pixar's *Inside Out.* There is a lot going on that cannot be seen from the outside.

• **How will we work with the covert processes at play during this change?** I have seen a dynamic of the good child and the bad child play out between superintendents and their principals. I have seen the old boys' network at play in the hiring of administrators. I have witnessed "conflict archeology" come to the surface years later in conversations when all of a sudden up for discussion was someone who worked for the district in the 1990s (!) who took away someone else's job 30 years ago. Unfortunately, but realistically, we are never just in the meeting in the present day by ourselves. We bring our histories with us to the present. I call it bringing "personal baggage" with you to the professional present. Make overhead bin space available because no one comes alone.

A few questions:

- Do I understand and accept that there may be unconscious reactions by individuals or groups as the result of hearing me speak?

- Do I know who might have the greatest anxiety in the room or be threatened most by what I will say?

- Do I have enough emotional or psychological intelligence and skills to be able to deal with—at least on some level—the basic unconscious defenses that I might encounter?

What's Really Going on Here?

According to Marshak (2006), covert processes are more often relationship related, emotionally based, and often out of awareness or unconscious, and defined by the group members as illegitimate or inappropriate.

Some typical covert issues in groups include:

- Feelings, emotions, and needs regarding power, inclusion, authority, intimacy, attraction, trust, or anger
- Fears, taboos, conflicts, and disagreements
- Aspirations, hopes, dreams, or spiritual values that are considered too far out or pie-in-the-sky
- Beliefs, norms, and cultural assumptions that guide and limit possibilities
- Unconscious dynamics such as projection, transference, denial, compensation, and group-based psychodynamics
- Deals, arrangements, understandings, and "politics" intended to advantage some over others
- Professional and personal biases and prejudices
- Unaddressed or unacknowledged differences based on culture, religion, gender, race, sexual orientation, physical ability, and styles

—From *Covert Processes at Work: Managing the Five Hidden Dimensions of Organizational Change,* Robert Marshak (2006)

The Turf Issue "Energy Trap"

Turf issues in departmentalized settings are examples of problems that will never go away. They are deeply rooted manifestations of territoriality, self-interest, and survival. The most useful question to ask is how can we work together compatibly holding service to students as our first priority while recognizing and honoring the needs or individual departments?

—From *The Adaptive School: A Sourcebook for Developing Collaborative Groups,* p. 194, Robert Garmston and Bruce Wellman (1999)

THE EVER-PRESENT ELEPHANT IN ORGANIZATIONS: RESISTANCE

When a change is being asked of a group, resistance is almost always a given. Not everyone will be upset, but it isn't realistic to think that someone won't be resistant. It's normal. Any organization, school, or district should be aware resistance will sprout up when change is on the horizon. And, if we know resistance is inevitable from the start, we must find ways to address the following concerns. These concerns should be addressed in the planning of any new initiative or change.

Some resistance can't be "fixed" in a conversation, but preparing oneself with the awareness that resistance will happen and how one handles the questions that will be asked goes a long way. Perhaps when a rollout of a new initiative is on the horizon, organizations can have an FAQ (Frequently Asked Questions) sheet prepared with answers to the following questions and concerns. Individuals will have their own worries and anxieties, but as a whole, the organization should be at the ready to engage in group-focused hard conversations.

FAQ SHEET ANSWERS TO HAVE PREPARED BEFORE A GROUP HARD CONVERSATION

- **Knowledge**—How will you be supporting others in understanding the change, and what it will entail in terms of shifts in their work?

- **Skills**—How will you be supporting others in gaining the skills to do the work?

- **Understanding of purpose**—How will you be supporting others through visuals, writing, speaking, and messaging as to the reason for this change and its purpose? Why is this change needed and/or required at this time?

- **Not having all involved in decision making**—How will you explain how the decision was made and who participated? Why were they the ones who were involved, and in what way can the others be involved as we move forward in the decisions that happen from now on?

- **Explaining what isn't okay with the way things are now**—How will you be explaining that status quo isn't okay for students or others? Do you have data or research that states the status quo isn't the right way to do business at this point?

- **Response to the statement, "We are doing too much already."**—How will you acknowledge that this change is in lieu of other work or is not truly going to take more time or what is coming off the plate?

- **Response to the question, "What are the benefits to changing?"**—How will you explain the benefits to changing for those who need to change and those who they are working with—students, colleagues, and so on?

- **Getting credible people to help with the change**—How will you find the right people to share the message, and how will you support those who aren't credible as of now to become more credible?

- **Response to the question, "Will support be offered?"**—How will you support the change? What funds, time, resources, support, coaching, and so on do you have planned for helping the change move forward?

- **Response to the statement, "We see a conflict with this new way of doing things and how we have done it in the past."**—How will you address this "elephant"? This is often a polarity management issue and requires helping others see that we aren't dismissing the old way *in its entirety* and instead offering specifics. How might you explain how this is not excluding all ways of how it has been done before so others don't feel "excommunicated" or completely disrespected?

- **Response to the statement, "This new way is in conflict with my personal values."**—How will you be professionally mindful of differing value systems in the room and name them? If it isn't a fait accompli say so. If it is, explicitly state it and acknowledge the difference and make sure others feel respected and aware of their choices and their freedom to make choices in their own careers.

- **Response to concerns of not being successful and failing and the reaction of administration if it doesn't go well immediately—** How will you address fear of failure and assure staff that the first year won't be evaluated or that supports are available? How are you building a continuous-growth mindset?

- **Expression of understanding with regard to negative experiences with change in the past—**How will you acknowledge past changes and what your contribution is to the inefficacy (if any) of that rollout and how will this time be different? Be specific. Take responsibility and ownership when you can.

During interactions with groups larger than two have the FAQ sheet described above at the ready. There are also some additional visual supports that you could use in order to make the delivery of challenging communications be more effective. In large groups, visuals are essential. A few ideas are outlined below.

GO VISUAL WITH GROUPS

Consider a Third Point

Put the data around which you are having a hard conversation *in front* of the group on a PowerPoint and then stand *with the group* looking at the PowerPoint, *not* aligning yourself with the PowerPoint. Standing closer *and in alignment with* the group (*all of you facing the data*) puts you in relationship *with* the group and not facing (i.e., *against)* the group. You are first point, the group is the second point, and the information is third point (hence the reference to the data being the "third point"). Separate yourself from the third point (i.e., teaching standards, expectations, student work, data), so the group sees you as someone to dialogue with *around* the set expectations and not as the enemy coming at them aligned *with* the information.

Consider a Fourth Point

In doing a session on a challenging topic that no one wants to discuss, you as the facilitator of this hard conversation can more safely mention "the elephants in the room" by pushing your palms out to the walls—to *outside* the room—while talking about it. Pushing the disturbing news "outside" makes the space for all who are inside a "safer" space. The bad news is pushed outside as a fourth point. Thus, no one is shamed or pointed out inside the room as thinking any of those feelings, yet "the elephant" is acknowledged.

Examples of how to acknowledge challenging issues with palms pushed toward the walls:

"Some might say . . ."

"It has been the experience in other schools that when this type of change happens that some have felt . . ."

"Others in the district outside this group have shared with me that . . ."

"I can imagine that in the past one might have heard . . ."

Then, once that fourth point has been expressed, *bring your palms down* and talk about what you want to address and your wish to do so together with the group inside the room. Believe me, this fourth point "dance" can work. For more amazing information on this "choreography" see *The Choreography of Presenting: The 7 Essential Abilities of Effective Presenters* by Kendall Zoller and Claudette Landry (2010).

As already stated, some resistance can't be fixed in a group conversation, but preparing oneself with the awareness that resistance will happen and how you respond goes a long way in addressing concerns.

SO WHAT IF YOU WANT TO HAVE A HARD CONVERSATION WITH A SUPERVISOR?

Organizational savvy is critical, and knowing what the dynamics could be as a systems hard conversation is key. Having a systems-level hard conversation requires an organizational savvy—a sense of knowing what is going on with the "higher ups" and thinking from their point of view as well as from your point of view. Support from "above" is critical in any rollout or implementation, so communicating to and with district supervisors in charge of a program is critical to supporting any implementation strategy. Yet we often fear talking to our boss. They have power. They could fire us! And, yet, if we don't speak up, the environment in which we work isn't healthy physically or emotionally, the project doesn't move along smoothly and could go south, and the students might not get what they need. We need to learn how to have hard conversations "up."

To speak up when you see things going wrong is challenging but *not* impossible. David L. Bradford, coauthor with Allan R. Cohen of *Influence Without Authority* and *Influencing Up* (Cohen & Bradford, 2012), has a few key insights (Freedman, 2013).

- Don't overexaggerate the power gap. When we do, we hurt ourselves and our bosses.

- Work on your influencing skills. When you frame your "want" in a way that also highlights the boss's and the organization's best interests, you can have a great deal of influence.

- Move beyond the concept of being a subordinate and, instead, be a junior partner. "Junior partner," while still recognizing the hierarchical difference, says "we are in the same boat together," so you are concerned for the boss's success as well as one's own.

Safety Is Not Comfort

Safety and comfort are not always the same thing in collaborative settings. Comfort with other people's discomfort is an important facilitator resource. It is not the facilitator's responsibility to make everyone feel at ease at all times. If groups are talking about the right things, individuals and the entire group may be unsettled at points in the conversation. The facilitator's responsibility is to protect the integrity of the process used and provide safety and security for group members by helping them trust that process.

—From *Data-Driven Dialogue: A Facilitator's Guide to Collaborative Inquiry*, Bruce Wellman and Laura Lipton (2004), p. 12

School-based educators share with me that they think the district office people are so different than they are. The district folks wear ties and pumps, and they talk to the board and the media. While roles are different, and a difference in responsibilities is clear, all of us are in these jobs to support students. As Bradford (Cohen & Bradford, 2012; Freedman, 2013) says, we hurt our administrators, as well as ourselves, when we aren't truthful. We need to see ourselves *on the same side* working toward a common goal. We need to be less afraid of our status and more concerned that we do right by our students.

Susan Ashford and James Detert (2015), authors of the *Harvard Business Review* article "Get the Boss to Buy In," pose excellent questions for us to consider before speaking up.

- What does my supervisor find most compelling about concerns? What convinces him or her to make changes? Money? Anecdotes? Data?

- How can I connect this issue to organizational priorities or other issues receiving attention?

- How can I highlight this change as an opportunity for the organization?

- What is the best moment to be heard by my supervisor? Can I catch the wave of a trend?

- What is the right time in the decision-making process to raise my issue? Is it now before things go too far or is it right at the point of "yea" or "nay"?

- How can I involve others in the department/office/unit effectively?

- Who will be potential blockers, and how can I persuade my boss to see the challenge as a worthy one to get into despite the resistance from his or her colleagues?

- Should I use a formal, public approach to sell my issue or an informal, private approach? A combination of the two?

- Am I suggesting a viable solution or at least moving in that direction? What do I propose as an alternative?

Speaking to Supervisors: Suggestions Not Expectations

Given the hierarchical nature of your relationship with your supervisor, you aren't in a position to put out a mandate or a non-negotiable command. You are in a position to offer recommendations and suggestions. Your "junior partner" status does not let you off the hook of thinking through solutions because "the boss should know what to do." Bring your best thinking to the conversation and as concerned as you are, as anxious

CHAPTER 4. ORGANIZATIONAL POLITICS, WORKING WITH SUPERVISORS

as you feel, try to speak with an approachable, suggestive tone. A few sentence stems that can bring your suggestions to the fore could include:

"One thing that might work . . ."

"There are a number of approaches . . . 1, 2, 3."

"A thought we should keep in mind is . . ."

"A few suggestions/recommendations could be to . . ."

You cannot say, "Here's how it is going to go down." You must allow your boss to make choices and save face. Strategic suggestions are a good first step.

"Sir, We Are Heading Toward an Iceberg, Sir"

My colleague, Phil, used to consult for the Navy. He said that when a subordinate saw something wrong—for example, the boat heading toward an iceberg—it was the responsibility of the subordinate to explain the problem to the officer not once, *but twice,* in order to be relieved of punishment.

If you are heading toward an "iceberg" and your boss cannot hear you, even with an adherence to the suggestions in this chapter, it is still your responsibility to share the news *at least twice.*

If you have shared your concern once and if something is still professionally unsound, physically unsafe, or emotionally damaging to staff or students, you need to share it again. Try these suggestions.

"Maybe the first time I brought this up it wasn't a great time to focus on it but it is still a challenge I think we need to address. Is this a better time?"

"I am still sitting with a discomfort (or lack of clarity) around how this initiative is being rolled out and I think we need to reconsider how we are going about doing so. Are you open for a discussion at this point?"

ONE LAST THOUGHT: WHEN YOUR ROLE IN THE ORGANIZATION INVOLVES MANAGING *OTHER* PEOPLES' CONFLICTS

As a team lead, department chair, supervisor, or administrator, you are often called upon to manage conflict. You might also have the responsibility to carry out directives that cause conflict. You are in charge of, at times, watching over the emotional needs of the group, providing support, and nurturing a culture of inclusiveness and collaboration. Tag, you're it.

If you are in charge of managing the change and need to mediate between two people or a department and an individual, there are some things you might need to do.

- Ask the individuals, "What are your concerns?" and listen. Some go away, while some represent challenges to be resolved. You might consider Outcome Mapping with the individuals as a way to get them to articulate what they see is the problem and what they want as outcomes. See Chapter 3.

- Separate yourself from the decision made from above that folks are having feelings about. Focus on the task of implementing the next steps of action and getting people in a future-focused mindset.

- Provide as much autonomy as you can for the individuals within the direction and constraints as defined.

- Model and, if need be, teach collaborative skills including discussion and dialogue to your colleagues.

- Provide tight, psychologically safe structures to talk about hard-to-talk-about topics.

There is great wisdom in the work of Kendall Zoller, Michael Grinder, Bruce Wellman, Laura Lipton, Robert Garmston, Diane Zimmerman, Learning Forward, the Thinking Collaborative, and all the experts who do amazing work managing groups and conflict. It is critical that we adopt the best skills of facilitation in all the settings in which we find ourselves having challenging conversations with groups—teachers, parents, or administrators. The bibliography below is just the beginning of a text study into finding ourselves more proficient in hard conversations at the organizational and group level.

THE CONVERSATION CONTINUES . . .

The Choreography of Presenting: The 7 Essential Abilities of Effective Presenters by Kendall Zoller and Claudette Landry, Corwin, 2010

Covert Processes at Work: Managing the Five Hidden Dimensions of Organizational Change by Robert Marshak, Berrett-Koehler Publishers, 2006

Data-Driven Dialogue: A Facilitator's Guide to Collaborative Inquiry by Bruce Wellman and Laura Lipton, MiraVia, 2004

"David L. Bradford: How Do You Manage Up in the Workplace?" by Michael Freedman, *Insights*, Stanford Graduate School of Business, October 8, 2013; http://www.gsb.stanford.edu/insights/david-l-bradford-how-do-you-man age-workplace

Get the Boss to Buy In by Susan Ashford and James Detert, *Harvard Business Review*, January/February 2015; https://hbr.org/2015/01/get-the-boss-to-buy-in/

Influencing Up by Allan R. Cohen and David Bradford, Wiley, 2012

Leading in a Culture of Change by Michael Fullan, Jossey-Bass, 2007

Lemons to Lemonade: Resolving Problems in Meetings, Workshops, and PLCs by Robert J. Garmston and Diane P. Zimmerman, Corwin, 2013

Scripting a Humane, Growth-Producing Conversation

5

The character of a man is known from his conversations.

—Menander

With our under-the-surface questions answered and our notes about what our look-fors are in our metaphorical back pocket (i.e., don't bring a full-on, filled-out action planning map to the hard conversation), we have the scaffold for our dialogue for our hard conversation. Having been allocentric and empathic in our thinking, we are more clear and professional in our problem statements and more compassionate and reasonable in our look-for behaviors. These understandings will hold us in good stead as we move toward scripting our initial thoughts.

In the book *Having Hard Conversations* (Abrams, 2009), six foundational parts of a script were spelled out. Over the years, I haven't altered my view that these six parts are essential when initiating a hard conversation. Miss one of these six parts and the communication is a bit empty and not as humane. There are additions, to be sure, but no real deletions. The six parts remain essential.

The six parts to a hard conversations initial script, in order, are as follows.

1. Setting the Tone

2. Naming the Issue

3. Giving Specific Examples

4. Clarifying the Impact

5. Making a Request for Action

6. Indicating a Request to Dialogue

These six basic parts are at the core of the scripting process. The art versus science of the script writing comes *after* you have scripted the basics and want to make the communication even more nuanced and personalized.

In this chapter as we consider our initial script, we want to stay allocentric and think about the recipient of our communication and how we will be heard. One of the best ways I have found to stay focused on how "the other" might receive the communication is to look at the script through the work of David Rock. Rock has created a frame for seeing threats and rewards that come up in any social interaction. He created what is known as the SCARF model.

SCARF MODEL

David Rock is a neuropsychologist and author of *Your Brain at Work: Strategies for Overcoming Distraction, Regaining Focus, and Working Smarter All Day Long* (2009). Among his many talents, Rock studies interactions and how each comment within an interaction can have a either a "push me or pull you" feel. One listens to someone as they share information and thinks, "Is this social encounter something I am going to enjoy or want to run away from? Even if I cannot run away, could I simply shut down? Is this conversation going to provide me with positive feedback, or will I leave this interaction feeling negative?" This "threat–reward" concept is a constant in all interactions, especially those taking place in professional learning communities, post-observations, or performance reviews. How will the recipient of the feedback feel about the interaction? Threatened or rewarded?

Your language can get in sync with the work of David Rock and the SCARF model he uses. And with it, you can write a hard conversation script that speaks to the threat–reward schema. Let's start with a bit of information about the SCARF model and then we can use it to write a more personalized script that will, hopefully, mitigate, and possibly eliminate, a few of the threat responses we as people can often feel in uncomfortable interactions.

Rock describes the SCARF model in a 2008 article in the *NeuroLeadership Journal*.

> [T]wo themes are emerging from social neuroscience. Firstly, that much of our motivation driving social behavior is governed by an overarching organizing principle of minimizing threat and maximizing reward (Gordon, 2000). Secondly, that several domains of social experience draw upon the same brain networks to maximize reward and minimize threat as the brain networks used for primary survival needs (Lieberman and Eisenberger, 2008). In other words, social needs are treated in much the same way in the brain as the need for food and water.

> The SCARF model summarizes these two themes within a framework that captures the common factors that can activate a reward or threat response in social situations. This model can be applied (and tested) in any situation

where people collaborate in groups, including all types of workplaces, educational environments, family settings and general social events.

The SCARF model involves five domains of human social experience: Status, Certainty, Autonomy, Relatedness and Fairness. . . . These five domains activate either the "primary reward" or "primary threat" circuitry (and associated networks) of the brain. (Rock, 2008, pp. 1)

The five domains Rock mentions in his work align with the acronym SCARF and are as follows:

Status is about relative importance to others.

Certainty is about the need to be able to predict the future.

Autonomy is a sense of choice and control over events.

Relatedness is a sense of safety with others, of friend rather than foe.

Fairness is a perception of how fair exchanges are between people.

Using SCARF for Scripting a Hard Conversation: Additions to Consider

Status—The importance of one's self compared to others/being of value

In the hard conversation, how might I ask myself and then acknowledge in the initial conversation—

- How long has this person been on staff
- What roles have they played while on staff
- What projects they led, or roles that they have done well

As I speak to my colleague, what can I do so he or she feels acknowledged for what he or she does, the level of expertise he or she has acquired, and the time frame in which they have continued to work for the organization?

Certainty—Ability to predict the near future

In the hard conversation, how might I ask myself and acknowledge in the initial conversation—

- How long this specific meeting will be
- The need one has to know regarding how the time frame for action and next steps
- What it would take to get an "A" in doing the next steps
- What additional steps need to be taken and what does not need to be done

As I speak to my colleague, what can I do so he or she is aware of the meeting time frame, the parameters of the conversation, and what needs to happen next?

(Continued)

(Continued)

Autonomy—Having some control over one's environment or actions

In this hard conversation, how might I ask myself and acknowledge in the initial conversation—

- What the other person can do "her way" and what needs to be done in a uniform way, like others in her role
- What is on this person's "plate" as a result of this conversation and what isn't—to give perspective
- What the time frame could be for next steps getting done and if there is any leeway with that time frame
- What could be said so this individual colleague feels capable of making choices—a comment about their capacity, their skills
- What I can say so the other person feels valued for his or her individual attributes

As I speak to my colleague, what can I do so he or she is clear about what is open for conversation and what is not up for discussion, what is hers to determine and what isn't, and how I value her expertise and contributions as a professional?

Relatedness—Being "in" or "out"—relating to social group, belonging, connection

In this hard conversation, how might I ask myself and acknowledge in the initial conversation—

- What this conversation means for this person in relation to everyone else in his or her group
- How this won't affect the person's "reputation" in the group and how the conversation will remain confidential, or how this might change the way the person could be viewed by others
- How I can treat my colleague like a colleague versus an adversary, appreciating what he or she has done and the history she has with me and the organization

As I speak to my colleague, what can I do so he or she sees that you understand his or her relationship to others and how this conversation or next steps might, in his or her mind, affect that group dynamic?

Fairness—Same rules and processes for everyone

In this hard conversation, how might I ask myself and acknowledge in the initial conversation—

- How this hard conversation is addressing something *all* staff in the school need to and are expected to do, not just this individual
- How this isn't the same for everyone; can I professionally state the reason for that perceived inequity so the person does not feel I am "out to get them"

As I speak to my colleague, what can I do so he or she feels this conversation is being had in a fair manner, in connection with contract and stated standards, and not being had exclusively with this person if it is a bigger conversation that should be had with the group?

In each of the sections of the script there are ways to create less of a threat by modifying language and creating a sense of awareness of the other person's perspective. Consider the person you are talking to. Has he been on staff for several decades? Might he need you to acknowledge his institutional history? Is she the union rep? Might you need to acknowledge the role that she plays? What additions into your script might you want to be more mindful of based on the SCARF domains? The SCARF concepts can be added into the script in a variety of places. It isn't about addressing the concepts in the right order or at the right time. There is no correct way to add the SCARF concepts into the script. The additions are to be personalized for the person to whom you will be talking. And yet, the script does have an initial order of parts and those parts lend themselves to specific SCARF additions.

The scripting protocol with the SCARF domains *embedded* into each of the six parts is below. Sentence stems expressing SCARF domains are provided after each part is described.

SIX-PART HHC SCRIPTING PROTOCOL WITH SCARF DOMAINS

1. Offer a reassuring statement regarding the meeting and set a respectful tone for the conversation.

(Choose to emphasize *status, relatedness, certainty.*) Acknowledge the person's role, your relationship to them, and so on.

> I appreciate you, and I hope you know that.
>
> We have worked together for more than a decade, right?
>
> You were here when . . . , correct? That is a lot of knowledge and institutional history.
>
> You have my respect for . . .

Continue by having the intention for conversation clarified and the time frame and agenda for the meeting (*certainty*). You might need to contrast here—meaning you want to provide context and proportion. . . . If this isn't the last straw, say so (*certainty*). You don't want the person to hear more than intended.

> This meeting is about . . .
>
> It isn't about you not being the chair of the department, not about not being back at this school.
>
> Just to contextualize this, this conversation isn't about (fill in the blank). Nor is it about (fill in the blank.)
>
> I want you to see the parameters about this conversation. It isn't about . . . It is only about . . .
>
> This is something important but not to be seen as final . . .

2. Name the issue.

Speak in professional language. Think facts and connect to standards, job description, and benchmarks that are already "on the books" and known by all in the organization. (Choose to emphasize *certainty* and *fairness*.)

Watch for "trigger" words that will threaten the listener. Avoid judgment calls, interpretations, or harsh adjectives in the statement of the issue (e.g., "Your class is chaotic," "You are difficult," or "You're viewed as being lazy"). No speculation either.

> This conversation is about your comments to the staff about compliance with the state requirements.
>
> I want to talk to you about the e-mail you sent to the whole staff about your frustration with the rollout of this initiative.
>
> I have observed your class twice in the last week and want to talk about the participation of your English learners.

Remember: If you haven't seen the issue you are discussing firsthand, you need to have *an investigatory conversation*, not a hard conversation. See sidebar for additional information.

Investigatory Versus Hard Conversations—Similarities and Differences

In some cases, you may need to bring up a difficult topic with someone as the supervisor, and yet you didn't witness the issue yourself. When you are going to ask someone about his or her behavior that you didn't see personally, you are having an *investigatory* conversation. These types of conversations are framed differently. Your purpose in an investigatory conversation is to gather information from the person about his or her perspective, and you must be clear that you were not the witness and are giving the individual some leeway.

"Julie, I want to talk to you about something I didn't personally witness but was told about. I appreciate your work with students, and you have always been a positive energy at our school, so I want to work with you to figure out what to do about . . ."

"Tom, I know that you are a gifted math teacher and certainly care about your students and what you teach. So I can imagine that you will also be upset to know about something said to me. I am hoping we can work together to sort this out . . ."

Be aware of when you are having an investigatory conversation rather than the hard conversations we will be working through here. The dialogue you are having in an investigatory conversation is tentative in language, firm but neutral. The conversation still needs to take place, but it needs to be done with both of you looking at the issue together as something to be "looked into."

—From *Having Hard Conversations,*
Jennifer Abrams (2009), p. 65

3. Select specific examples that illustrate the behavior or situation you want to change.

Too many examples will increase the threat level for the individual. If there is a pattern and you can describe as succinctly as possible, do so. From looking at scripts over the last few years, it is appropriate to provide two or three current examples and to be extremely factual. Remember the difference between evidence and opinion. More than three examples and the individual feels kick-boxed. (Choose to emphasize *certainty.*)

You have mentioned aloud in the staff lounge how what we are doing is "terrible for kids" and how this isn't "real teaching" and how "this is stupid paperwork."

You wrote in the e-mail that this initiative is a "waste of your time" and your colleagues' time and that it must have been thought up by those who "clearly don't know what teaching is."

The four English learners I watched in class over two 45-minute periods didn't speak to other students or raise their hands when asked whole-group questions. Two of them started to speak to each other and you shushed them by saying, "Stay focused."

Possible Addition to the Script

Caution: At this point, describe your feelings regarding this issue *only* if you feel it is appropriate to share them. If it is an interpersonal issue between you and your colleague and it is necessary to share, it is reasonable to bring your feelings to the conversation. (Choose to emphasize *relatedness.*) Is this an interpersonal hard conversation? Are you feeling disrespected by something the person said to you or about you? Are you feeling you didn't receive credit for something you did? Do you feel justified in sharing, "I felt disrespected," or "I felt dismissed"? It makes good sense to add feelings to the conversation when the concern is about you and your relationship with the other person.

It is a different ballgame when you are talking about your colleague's actions that *aren't* interpersonal in nature. These possible additions are the comments that have a tendency to move the conversation in such a way that moves the focus off the topic and on to *you*. You could be the wrong person on which to be concentrating energy and time and focus. E-mails to members of the team are not personal for you if you aren't on the team. The same for meeting of organizational deadlines. Consider *not* using feelings in these types of conversations. Adding yourself to the conversation at this stage triangulates the conversation and the person needs to focus energy solving the problem, not on making your relationship better. You wouldn't say, for example, "I was so bored observing your class today. I am horrified the district hired you to teach this subject," or "I really dislike having to cover for you when parents call the office," as the subject of the conversation is not you.

> When you wrote the whole-school e-mail, I felt disrespected as a fellow educator as you commented, albeit indirectly, that admin doesn't know what teaching is and that blanket statement included me.
>
> As a teacher for more than a decade that comment hurt me.

Two Examples of When *Not* to Add Your Feelings to the Conversation

Example 1

An assistant principal received calls—three in number—from parents who were upset with a teacher not posting grades in a timely manner. The assistant principal took the calls over the course of the week. When it was evident this had become a pattern, she went to the teacher to address the situation. As she shared with the teacher the need for her grades to be posted in a timely manner and then the assistant principal added that she was also personally frustrated that she had to "cover" for this teacher and "waste her work time" taking phone calls from angry parents. She wanted the teacher to know how much of a "pain" this had been for her personally.

We have all felt frustrated and burdened with "emergencies" that are not of our making. The assistant principal had taken on a role in which parent phone calls would be a part her everyday work life. The insertion of her frustration into the conversation didn't help the teacher put her grades online more quickly. It triangulated the process by having the teacher need to balance making the assistant principal feel better *and* put her grades up online. Not productive.

Example 2

An administrator wanted to add a sentence or two of shame into the hard conversation script she brought to a workshop. Making the other person feel shame during her script made sense to her based on her background and how shame had been used effectively in her upbringing. She wanted the teacher to feel a similar sense of guilt. Her supervisee had let her down and she should feel bad about it. Not only did the behavior in the classroom need to change, but this teacher, in her administrator's eyes, had done something outside the norms of acceptability and she should feel bad.

If made to feel shame, certain people *will* change. However, it isn't everyone's go-to response. Some educators, who are anti-authority, would be infuriated to now be asked feel bad because the boss makes them feel bad. Being asked to feel shame is too familial in nature for some within in a professional context. Feelings can be tricky. They should be shared, depending on the context, or if shared, can backfire on you. Be mindful.

4. Clarify what the impact is on others, the person, the school or class, and so on.

(Choose to emphasize *relatedness.*) Is there a long-term consequence that is not recognized, such as students won't have what they need in terms of knowledge for next year and it isn't understood by this person? Or is there way the community might see this situation that the person might not see? Or is there a ripple effect of a number of people who are impacted as a result of this person's actions and the person is truly unaware? State the reason you are having this conversation. What might the person not see about his or her impact on others?

The impact of your words on the staff is that of bringing resistance to the work instead of engagement. I am not suggesting you don't have a right to your feelings. I am speaking about the impact your comments have on morale.

When your comments are written and then sent to the whole school instead of being addressed to those with whom you have disagreements, it changes the conversation from dealing with the initial issue to also having to deal with a whole-staff communication and it was unnecessary to move it to that level.

When any of our students aren't asked to engage in speaking activities it limits their opportunities to learn, especially those who are English learners and who explicitly need every opportunity to become fluent in the language. It is a missed opportunity.

Possible Addition to the Script

Caution: Identify your contribution to this problem only if you feel it will be useful in this conversation. (Choose to emphasize *relatedness.*)

It does take two to tango. We should own up to our actions or our inaction if it will move the conversation into a place of dialogue and future thinking. Acknowledging your role in this conversation can be helpful. There are times the other person needs you to say, "I wasn't clear," or "I didn't address this in the way I could have," or "We didn't follow through as we could have." Authentic declarations that speak to your contributions are welcome.

And, sometimes you didn't contribute to the problem, so an acknowledgment *isn't* warranted. You are not in charge of doing another person's tasks (e.g., getting to school on time). Some things aren't yours to own. Determine what is "on your side of the net" and what isn't.

If you had a role in this situation/issue, bring it up now. Do not bring up your responsibility to the situation if you feel that the person will simply say, "Then it is your problem," and not take ownership of their part of the solution. Sometimes sharing your contribution shows you are in it together and it creates a sense of relatedness and collegiality. At other times, it could push all the responsibility back on you and the person won't own his or her part of the problem and how he or she needs to be part of the solution.

Then it becomes *your* problem. Knowing what is yours and what isn't is key. Don't own what isn't yours.

> I will take responsibility for how the initial communications about the initiative were stated.
>
> I now know they didn't give the group enough time to respond. I own that.
>
> I now know the wording put off a few individuals. I am sorry for how it was stated.

5. Indicate your wish to dialogue and resolve the issue, and give specifics as to how it needs to be or could be resolved.

What needs to happen next? What is a must? What could be negotiated? What choices can the individual make about how he or she can change behavior? What is absolute? What is up for discussion? (Choose to emphasize *certainty* and *autonomy*.) Are there specific action steps this person could take starting now? What behaviors might this person start doing that would resolve this problem? If there are many actions to take, might you summarize for now and then go into the specifics as you begin to dialogue?

> I want to talk with you when you feel something isn't done right or communicated well. Whenever you want to do so, let me know. What cannot happen is that whole-staff e-mails be sent when it isn't a whole-staff discussion.
>
> You know the students well and I respect your groupings and your choices of activities and all students need to participate in them. If that means additional supports need to be in place or activities need to be modified for the English learners, the modifications need to be created by you and included in instruction. It is essential for their learning.

6. Conclude this part of the conversation and invite your partner to start a dialogue.

If you want to know your colleague's opinion, ask for it. If you want to hear her thoughts, tell her. You could also say, "Let me know if you see this differently." If you need to end with "Do you understand?" be clear about that too. You could thank your colleague for letting you speak and now you are you are hoping you two can have a conversation about next steps (choose to emphasize *relatedness*). You might ask, "Given that this is a non-negotiable (choose to emphasize *certainty*) but many ways to get it done (choose to emphasize *autonomy*), what are you thinking is a good next step?" The goal of this last statement is to move into the conversation and setting it up with a respectful, productive question or statement that moves the conversation along.

> Given that the compliance issues aren't going away, would you like to talk about strategies to make it easier for you to manage the work?
>
> Can you see this from the administration's perspective?
>
> Given that it is a requirement we provide supports, what help do you need to create those lessons?

AT LAST: HOW DO I CONCLUDE THE CONVERSATION?

As the conversation concludes, what do you want to make sure gets said *before* the conversation ends? How will you sum up? How will you restate what has been learned? Will you send something to the person via e-mail? Set up another time? Mention action plan items from your outcome map (choose to emphasize *certainty*)?

> I want to give you time to think, and if you have some ideas of how we can move through the compliance paperwork more smoothly let me know. We want to make it easier. I will find you next week, okay?
>
> I appreciate you seeing this from our perspective. Thank you. It means a lot to me to have us working together for the sake of students.
>
> Let me send you the list of strategies we talked about, and I am happy to provide additional support, coaching, books, and so on. Just ask. Thanks for being willing to think with me.
>
> I know this has been challenging. I appreciate that we were able to have this type of conversation and talk about what's best for the students. I will send you an e-mail reiterating some next steps and a summary, and I will check in with you in the next week or so. Thank you.
>
> I continue to be glad we are working together and I am glad to be able to be candid and upfront. I hope you see I don't take these conversations lightly and am grateful that you engaged with me. Your comments were powerful and have left me thinking as well.

I believe there are a few absolutes to include as the conversation concludes:

- A show of respect (reconnect with *status* and *relatedness*)

- An appreciation for the person's interest in the work and the students' success (holding the vision, the expectations of the work, and recognizing the bigger picture) (*fairness*)

- Some information about the next steps (emphasizing *certainty* or *autonomy,* depending on the situation)

THREE LAST THOUGHTS AS YOU PREPARE YOUR SCRIPT

1. What if I anticipate the person will interrupt me?

If you think that the person will be interrupting, try to preempt it by telling the person at the beginning that you have something to say and you would like to say it all the way through. It might take 60–90 seconds to get your idea across. It won't be a monologue; you do want to dialogue but want to share a full thought first. If the person then interrupts, you have tried to set a public agreement. You restate that public agreement and then continue.

2. Why is it so important I keep it short?

The shorter and clearer your statements are, the sooner the person can process and give you more information that may help you help him or her. In "How Do You Know If You Talk Too Much?" Mark Goulston (2015) says after 20 seconds you should check to see if you can continue. Get eye contact or confirmation with body language they are still with you. After 40 seconds, you might be considered long-winded and the other person might be building up resistance or hurt. So be mindful of your expounding on the subject just to gain authority or power. Be humane and as succinct as possible.

3. What if I feel bad about having to have the conversation?

Smothering, excusing, apologizing, and getting in the way of someone else's thinking with a hug or your voice won't be as helpful as being quiet and providing a space for them to take in the comments. No enabling.

We are preparing for a conversation with a colleague, an adult. We need to allow them to be independent and respond as they can. We can show care and accountability. Be humane and growth-producing. Be compassionate and clear. It can be done.

THE CONVERSATION CONTINUES . . .

Changing on the Job: Developing Leaders for a Complex World by Jennifer Garvey Berger, Stanford Business Books, 2013

"How Do You Know If You Talk Too Much?" by Mark Goulston, *Harvard Business Review Blog*, June 3, 2015; https://hbr.org/2015/06/how-to-know-if-you-talk-too-much/

Leading Adult Learning: Supporting Adult Development in Our Schools by Ellie Drago-Severson, Corwin, 2009

Learning for Leadership: Developmental Strategies for Building Capacity in Our Schools by Ellie Drago-Severson and Jessica Blum-DeStefano, Corwin, 2013

"SCARF: A Brain-Based Model for Collaborating With and Influencing Others" by David Rock, *NeuroLeadership Journal*, 2008; http://www.davidrock.net/files/NLJ_SCARFUS.pdf

"Tell Me So I Can Hear—A Developmental Approach to Feedback and Collaboration" by Ellie Drago-Severson and Jessica Blum-DeStefano, *JSD*, December 2014

Your Brain at Work: Strategies for Overcoming Distraction, Regaining Focus, and Working Smarter All Day Long by David Rock, Harper Business, 2009

What If They Say . . . ? 6

Possible Responses

What gives light must endure burning.

—Viktor Frankl

You use all the learnings from this book. You speak with the utmost humanity. You are mindful of other peoples' need for acknowledgment, autonomy, and affiliation. You stay on "your side of the net." And sometimes, it still isn't enough. The other person doesn't appreciate your intentions or listen with an interest in meeting you halfway. Instead, they get mean. They scream. They attack your personality. They attack the school, the district, and the world. How do you respond?

I often wished that I could marshal my words at moments like these, instead of "going small" and retreating. Many of us Gen Xers and Boomers remember a doll called Chatty Cathy who would speak when you pulled the chatty ring in its upper back. How I wish I too could just pull a Chatty Cathy ring and say the right thing! It isn't always possible. And, yet, we can prepare ourselves for moments like those mentioned above.

In this chapter, I have posed several questions that have been asked of me: the "What if they say . . . ?" questions. My responses might not be an exact fit for your unique context. No doubt, all responses need to be modified to fit your style, your context, the person to whom you are talking, and your school or organization. The responses are a *starting* point. Mark Goulston, author of a *Harvard Business Review* blog, "Don't Get Defensive: Communication Tips for

> Trying to help someone who comes to you already angry with other issues and needs an immediate resolution can be daunting. Finding the right words without being condescending or escalating the issue is always a challenge, especially when you are not a person who is quick-thinking (which I am not).
>
> —School Secretary, Maine

the Vigilant" (2013), might call these comments "controlled confrontation" responses. Use them as ideas to work with; to push back at; to rewrite. Make them work for you.

CONFLICT RESPONSES

When you are intimidated by someone shouting, name-calling, swearing, threatening:

"I am open to having this conversation, and I know you are angry. However, I will not continue talking with you if you speak at that volume, swear at me, or use that language. Please stop or we cannot continue the conversation."

"I am having difficulty hearing your message because your tone of voice is too harsh for me to listen to. Would you please state your need in a more neutral tone?"

"You have every right to feel that way, but no right to express it in an offensive manner. Please restate your objection in a more polite way."

When someone responds with general words like "never," "always," or "every time" instead of talking about a specific situation:

"While it may seem true that this happens 'all the time' or that I never respond, the truth is that is not true. It's an overgeneralization. Let's try to focus this conversation on *this* specific situation . . ."

When someone attacks your personality or identity instead of trying to solve the problem:

"We need to focus on issues rather than personalities. If you can return to the issue at hand, we can continue this important discussion. Otherwise I am going to ask that we stop now."

When someone brings things up from the past that have nothing to do with the present conflict:

"I understand that there were experiences prior to this one that you feel have a connection with what we are talking about. At this point, that information isn't the focus of this *current* conversation. Let's direct our attention to this *specific* situation."

When someone brings something up that is valid, but a completely different topic:

"I see two different topics are starting to be at play in this conversation. And I am not discounting your point. Both topics are important. Can we start with the topic we first started discussing and then, if we want, we go back to discuss the other?"

When someone refuses to listen and acts as if this issue isn't worth talking about:

"From your vantage point, this might not seem like it is worthy of discussion. However, the impact this action has had on others has made it difficult to . . ./challenging for _____ to do their job. I have a responsibility to bring it up and as a professional on the team, you have a responsibility to engage with this information."

When someone wants to be let off the hook:

"Everyone is responsible for this work. While I understand your circumstances (share details), I also understand the need for the student (or the program) that this be finished. What can I do to support you, because I am committed to making sure the work is done? Do you have some ideas as to how you can move forward?"

When someone needs to push past the letter of the law to the spirit of the law:

"I acknowledge you have done (explain what has been done). And as it was written, the expectation was 'fulfilled.' And, going beyond the expectation as it was spelled out in these ways (explain) would have this impact (on your colleagues, on the students, on the school). Here is a next step that would really make the work go up a notch in quality. (Explain). Is that doable?"

When someone says, "They don't treat us like professionals":

"Many professions, ours included, have standards and are constantly held accountable to changing expectations and the newest research. Think about doctors and tax accountants and pilots. They are held responsible to doing the work in alignment with the latest findings or policies. Professionals hold each other accountable to doing what is best practice. And holding ourselves up to standards is a professional practice."

When someone says, "The district always makes us . . .":

"We are the district. All of us. I am included. If you are talking about the district office administration, that is another issue, and yet we all have a voice. We can always ask our colleagues for clarification, seek support, and ask that those working there address concerns we have. But stating that 'the district' is making us do something gives away our power. We have a sphere of control and influence."

When someone says, "They don't give us enough time . . .":

"I don't disagree. There isn't enough time. I have found myself feeling the same way. I have found that this modification helped me make some time. . . .

(add suggestion) . . . and when I did the positive impact was (share impact). And given that we did all agree that this was an expectation and that it isn't going off the table, what do you suggest what we do next?"

When someone who is doing the work is frustrated with others who aren't "on board" and angry you haven't said anything:

"It is frustrating when we feel that we are doing more than others are doing. Our fairness antenna is triggered. I relate. I might suggest you talk to the individuals yourself. We as professionals need to hold each other accountable to doing the work, and we are collectively responsible for getting it done. Do you want some suggestions for how to talk to your colleague?"

When someone has really triggered you:

"Let's each take a breath here because I'm feeling really reactive, and I know until I calm down a bit whatever I say or do now will only make this conversation worse."

When someone says "You have it out for me! You want me to fail!":

"That is patently false. I do not have it out for you nor do I want you to fail. I want you to succeed, and I want the students to succeed too. I am committed to helping you and offering you help, and I am also committed to making sure the students are taken care of and that we don't fail them. Let's talk about how you can succeed."

When someone says, "You know I have a point! I am right" (and they are):

"You're right. You're correct. This isn't okay. This _____ was done poorly. And, I too am right. (State the facts on your end.) And you too have a responsibility from where you sit to be a part of the solution. I don't disagree that this hasn't moved along the way it should have. The process could have been a better one. And, we still need to get to the result. I will agree that . . . Will you also agree . . . ?"

When someone says, "You are always in the weeds. You don't see the big picture":

"We definitely see things from different perspectives and from different places. There is validity in looking at the bigger picture. It helps the district see where we have been and where we are going. It is your job to be up there looking at the organization at that level.

For some of us, we are doing the work of implementing that vision and the focus on detail we need to have is different. The 'micro' matters. We need to pay attention to precision and accuracy at our level, and it would be helpful if you didn't call this way of thinking 'being in the weeds,' but instead 'focusing on the details.'"

Or moving someone to the "forest level" when all they can see is the "tree level":

"You are asking great detail questions. Let's look at the big picture for a minute. So if we were looking at things from the balcony and not the dance floor, another valid way to look at this would be . . . and it isn't wrong to see it from this perspective as well."

When someone says, "You are so emotional":

"I am emotional because I care deeply about this issue. I realize my tone and my volume can be a bit 'much' for some, and I will take a look at how my style might get in the way of getting my point across. But I won't apologize for my level of concern when it comes to _____ because it is too important of a concern to be dismissed."

When someone says, "How can you change her? She's always been like that":

"I am not discounting that _____ 's personality can be really difficult to deal with. And, we need to speak to her about her impact on others. Her personality isn't the topic of conversation, as personalities are hard to change. Instead, we are discussing specific behaviors; how behaviors impact our ability to work well together. Behaviors can change, and I would like to address concerns about her behavior."

What if someone makes a racist, sexist, or homophobic comment?

Instead of avoiding racist, sexist, homophobic, anti-Semitic, Islamophobic, or negative generalized statements, you might want to address uncomfortable, untrue comments when they're made by using one or more of the following "Seize the Moment" responses.

- "Tell me more about what makes you say that."

- "I'm not willing to agree with that generalization."

- "Do you think that's true generally? Do you have a specific student or example in mind?"

- "Some of the words you just used make me uncomfortable."

- "That seems unfair to me."

- "I have a different opinion."

- "Here's an example of how I feel differently."

If you can say nothing else, say "Ouch."

And if you can say nothing else, say "Ouch." My colleague, Letitia Burton, always said, "Ouch," when she felt triggered or hurt or angry and didn't have the next word at the ready. "Ouch" truly says so much in so little space, allows for a pause in the conversation, doesn't let someone off the hook, and helps you to feel like you did speak up.

I am not a Trekkie, but I do appreciate a comment from the character Lieutenant Tuvok from *Star Trek: Voyager.* Lieutenant Tuvok said something wise: "Do not mistake composure for ease." This response work isn't easy. You might not feel comfortable responding to these types of comments, but with the awareness that you aren't the only one who is confronted with these challenging situations and with the knowledge that there *are* ways to respond with composure, you have a better chance to be the professional you want to be.

THE CONVERSATION CONTINUES . . .

"Don't Get Defensive: Communication Tips for the Vigilant" by Mark Goulston, *Harvard Business Review,* November 15, 2013; https://hbr.org/2013/11/dont-get-defensive-communication-tips-for-the-vigilant

Lemons to Lemonade: Resolving Problems in Meetings, Workshops, and PLCs by Robert J. Garmston and Diane P. Zimmerman, Corwin, 2013

How to Be a Better Recipient of Feedback 7

One of the greatest gifts is that of being good at disappointment: having non-persecutory, speedy, resilient emotional digestion.

—Alain de Botton

This whole book centers on you either being the person initiating, planning, and delivering a hard conversation, and to responding to challenging comments that come your way. Yet there is also *another* challenging piece to the hard conversation experience: the listening to difficult comments or perspectives that come your way about your behavior and your actions. In this chapter the focus is on being the *receiver* of challenging feedback.

Gulp. Feedback is coming. Get ready. Professional learning communities have given us opportunities to look collectively at data and see our impact. Sometimes it's not easy to do. Walk-throughs, video recordings, and post-observation discussions allow us to review statistics, hear quotations, and see our actions. Evaluations from colleagues are written after delivering professional development sessions. Parents share their perspectives on their child's schooling, and students fill out end-of-semester feedback forms. We get lots of feedback. And sometimes we hear some information that hurts. If possible, and we know ahead of time, we might ready ourselves to hear challenging feedback.

> Others' views of you are input, not imprint. It's information, not damnation.
>
> —Douglas Stone and Sheila Heen, *Thanks for the Feedback: The Science and Art of Receiving Feedback Well* (2014)

Emotions at Play: Statistics About Feedback

The amount of time we need to recover from negative emotions can differ as much as 3,000% across individuals (Davidson & Begley, 2002).

About 50% of our happiness is wired in. Another 40% can be attributed to how we interpret and respond to what happens to us, and 10% is driven by our circumstances. Whether these are exactly the right proportions is obviously debatable, but what's certain is that there is a lot of room to move in that magic middle of around 40% (Stone & Heen, 2014).

STRATEGIES FOR LISTENING MORE EFFECTIVELY TO FEEDBACK

What are the best practices for being more resilient and having "speedy emotional digestion"? The practices are categorized into what you can do to psychologically prepare, physically ready yourself, and verbally respond during hard conversations. See what works for you.

Psychological

- Before you go into a situation you expect to be difficult, ground yourself. Deep breaths. Connect yourself to the earth.

- Create an oval "bubble" of a strong boundary around you—at least one arm's length in front, behind, and on either side of you. Stand firmly in this protective bubble, and do not let the energy of others penetrate the bubble. Hear the words, but keep a sense of self.

- Remember, different cultures listen and give feedback differently—be understanding when feedback is given to you in a way that doesn't fit your style. Work to hear "beyond style." Try to accommodate to the styles of others.

- Friend failure, don't become it. I have heard many people say, "I'm such a failure." You, yourself, do not *equate to failure*. Be wary of labeling yourself.

- Remember to be in Martin Seligman's (2006) *Learned Optimism* "state of mind." Don't globalize, localize. This was one time and it doesn't mean it will *always* be this way. Don't catastrophize.

- Continually work on building of Carol Dweck's (2007) "growth mindset." Don't be fixed in your thinking. Everything can be a learning experience. We can always be growing. You are never done learning.

- During the conversation, when you notice you are being triggered (perhaps you notice a nervousness in your stomach or tension in your jaw), say hello to the reaction in you, and *invite it to sit beside you* until the conversation is over. Instead of acting out, you can put the reaction on hold until you have the time and space to nurture it properly. With the time and space you need later, you can learn about what caused that reaction to arise and how you might work with it in the future (from work at http://www.focusing.org/).

Physical

• Eat well. Sleep as much as you need. When you are physically depleted, you feel things in a different, more highly charged way. Think of yourself functioning with jet lag—dragging, sleepy, emotional, cranky. If you know you are going into a challenging week, don't be emotionally jet lagged. Be prepared.

• Practice the "Wonder Woman" pose. Watch Amy Cuddy's TED Talk (2012; http://www.ted.com/speakers/amy_cuddy) and then practice a Wonder Woman pose before a challenging meeting where you anticipate difficult feedback. Cuddy, a social psychologist at Harvard Business School, has done research on how, by placing ourselves in specific stances and body positions, we can change our own body chemistry to feel more confident and change other people's perceptions of our credibility.

• Use Stanford Graduate School of Business Professor Deborah Gruenfeld's (2013) "Playing High" body language. If you feel you need more credibility in the moment, try the following actions.

    o Keep a still head
    o Speak in complete sentences
    o Hold eye contact while talking
    o Move smoothly
    o Occupy maximum space
    o Lean back
    o Slow down
    o Spread body to full comfort
    o Look down (tilt head back a bit)

• If you are concerned about being viewed as too rigid and authoritarian, use Professor Gruenfeld's (2013) "Playing Low" body language. "Lower" your authority by changing body positions and becoming more approachable.

    o Nod in agreement
    o Smile even when it's not funny (fake smile showing top teeth)
    o Put hands near face while speaking
    o Sound breathless or start sentences with "um"
    o Speak haltingly and in incomplete sentences, edit as you go, trail off
    o Take up as little space as possible; space constrains body
    o Briefly check out the other person's eyes, looking for understanding and acknowledgment
    o Look up at other, tilt head down
    o Lean forward to check other person's responsiveness

• If you are taken by surprise, take two *deep* breaths. Get oxygen to your brain.

• If you fear you are going to cry, tighten up below the waist. Your focus will go downward and you will clench below the waist, physiologically changing your energy and moving energy away from your face and eyes. Tensing up your lower body gives you a stronger posture as well.

• If you are concerned you are going to get emotional, either with anger or tears, don't look down. Looking down has you moving into feelings. Look up to the ceiling and it will take you to a more neutral space.

• If you are feeling a bit out of control, sip water or coffee to give yourself a second to get your brain in a space to respond. Bring a water bottle to the meeting and hold it for groundedness.

• Put a mint in your cheek to stay in the moment. Physically stay in your body.

• Breathe like a seasoned negotiator. The rate and pace of your breathing affects your energy and also your general susceptibility to neuroses. Yawning a lot before a tête-à-tête can calm you down. Perform the act right before a hard conversation.

• Speak with a deeper voice. High-pitched voices are annoying because they activate a range of sound waves that requires more brainwork to interpret. Studies have shown that high-pitched voices convey a lack of effectiveness. The last two strategies are from *Five Strange Workplace Conversation Tips From a Hostage Negotiator* by Natalie Kitroeff (2015).

• Think about being "Velcro" with positive statements and "Teflon" with negative comments. The negative words won't seep into your psyche as easily. (Thanks to Andrea Stringer for the metaphor.)

Verbal

• When someone says, "Can I give you some feedback?" say, "I am open to feedback and respond best when it is humane and growth producing." It will most likely stop them from saying something that is too off the cuff and won't be kind.

• You have permission to ask for clarification. If it is fuzzy, ask for clarity. If you don't understand, ask for more detail. Remember your tone but ask for clarification.

And If the Feedback Still Stings . . .

• Try a self-compassion or loving-kindness (metta) meditation. Sharon Salzberg (www.sharonsalzberg.com) and Kristin Neff (www.self-compassion. org) both are self-compassion researchers, authors, and teachers.

• Give yourself what Stone and Heen (2014) call a "second score." The other person's initial evaluation of you is not the end of the story. It is how you took a "shot at figuring out what there is to learn" that also matters.

• Journal after the experience and ask yourself these questions:

   o What did you do to be professional and mature?
   o What would you do differently next time?
   o What did you learn that was new in this conversation?

How will you be more empowered to have a difficult conversation in the future?

Julian of Norwich, an important Christian mystic, has taken me through many a rough patch of processing difficult feedback with her comment, "All shall be well and all shall be well and all manner of things shall be well." Input, not imprint. We grow with each conversation.

THE CONVERSATION CONTINUES . . .

Bounce [web log] by Bobbi Emel; www.thebounceblog.com, www.bobbieemel.com, @bobbiemel

The Culture Map: Breaking Through the Invisible Boundaries of Global Business by Erin Meyer, Public Affairs, 2014

The Emotional Life of Your Brain: How Its Unique Patterns Affect the Way You Think, Feel and Live—and How You Can Change Them by Richard Davidson with Sharon Begley, Hudson Street Press, 2002

"Five Strange Workplace Conversation Tips From a Hostage Negotiator" by Natalie Kitroeff, 2015; http://www.bloomberg.com/news/articles/2015-03-30/five-strange-workplace-conversation-tips-from-a-hostage-negotiator

The Language of Emotions: What Your Feelings Are Trying to Tell You by Karla McLaren, Sounds True, 2010

Learned Optimism: How to Change Your Mind and Your Life by Martin Seligman, Vintage, 2006

Mindset: The New Psychology of Success by Carol Dweck, Ballantine, 2007

Self-Compassion: The Proven Power of Being Kind to Yourself by Kristin Neff, William Morrow, 2011

Power & Influence [Video file] by Deborah H. Gruenfeld, 2013; http://leanin.org/education/power-influence

Thanks for the Feedback: The Science and Art of Receiving Feedback Well by Douglas Stone and Sheila Heen, Viking/Penguin, 2014

Conclusion

It is not your responsibility to finish the work of perfecting the world, but you are not free to desist from it either.

—Rabbi Tarfon, Pirke Avot 2:21

Giving feedback. Getting feedback. Our journey of adult learning is long and can be supportive and helpful or painful and wounding. What motivates? What demotivates? Studying the fields of neuroscience, organizational effectiveness, leadership, and mindfulness helps us recognize how much influence we can have on each other, our productivity, and our contentment in the workplace. We need to strive to better understand ourselves, understand one another, and understand how organizations function in order to be successful in our hard conversations. We might have gotten into the field to teach students but we need to "grow" the adults as well.

Linda Lambert, author of *Building Leadership Capacity in Schools* (1998) and *Leadership Capacity for Lasting School Improvement* (2003) offers us several adult learning assumptions that we need to be mindful of as we have hard conversations with our colleagues, our supervisors, and our supervisees.

1. **Adults have a drive toward competence, which is linked to self-image and efficacy.** We don't want to look bad. No matter if we are 83 or 33, self-image matters. We want to look competent, feel capable, and be in control. Hearing challenging feedback can give us the impression we aren't smart or capable. We must always honor our colleague's dignity and respect them as a human being.

2. **Learning is both an opportunity and a risk; it requires dissonance and change.** Dweck's (2007) work on the growth mindset is ever-present in the work we do with students. We need to honor "the learning stretch" of adults in our schools as well. There is discomfort in being either party in a hard conversation. There is dissonance and risk in speaking up. No matter one's age, it takes courage to change. I wish at 48 years of age it was easier for me to speak up but, alas, I am learning to live in the gray and the "uncomfortableness." I am working on dealing with ambiguity and discomfort every day.

3. **Learning is the continual process of identity formation, or growing into more of who we are becoming.** One of my favorite stories is of my former superintendent who, on his first day in his new job, stood in front of 750 of us and said, "I woke up this morning and thought, 'Hot dang. I'm the Sup.'" It was a vulnerable moment. Authentic and telling. No matter who we are and what position we hold, we are always growing in our identities. So many moments to feel like an imposter. Sometimes we just need to act in order to discover who we are in this work as educators.

In summary, consider these key ideas from the book as you think about your hard conversations to come.

- Should I have a cease and desist conversation, a clarifying conversation, or a hard conversation?

- Has this become too personal or affective in nature? Can I frame this in a more professional way and take it out of being too emotional in how I speak about it? Can I get more neutral in how I speak of the challenge?

- When I think about the planning of this conversation, have I determined what I want as an outcome and the look-for behaviors I will share if I need to get detailed in my action plan?

- Have I thought about my filters of perception and how I view the work and how that might be different from my colleagues (culture, gender, mindset)? Does understanding where he or she might be coming from assist me in being more compassionate and strategic in my wording?

- Have I thought through how I would script the initial parts to the conversation, taking into consideration the SCARF threat-reward model and how speaking to status, certainty, autonomy, relatedness, and fairness might help the conversation be heard more effectively?

- Do I have a few responses ready if the person responds with anger or resentment, and are those responses both assertive in tone and humane in phrasing?

- Have I prepared myself for being challenged by difficult feedback and used a few of the strategies to ready myself for some discomfort?

- Do I know in my being that getting "into trouble, necessary trouble" could be the next best right thing to do if something is educationally unsound, physically unsafe, or emotionally damaging? Am I willing to do so?

This isn't cookie-cutter work. It is incredibly complex and nuanced, but a set of questions such as those offered above, and the inspirational quotes in the following Resource, can provide a sense of support and encouragement that gives us the confidence and the courage to move forward. And you always have me to talk to as well. Find my contact information in the About the Author section.

F. Scott Fitzgerald said, "Being grown up is a terribly hard thing to do. It is much easier to go from one childhood to another." The characters in his novels might have stayed immature and childish, but we educators are in the real world with real children whom we must love deeply and teach well. We, the adults, need to understand that while our own learning can be difficult, and that hard conversations are challenging, we can't let ourselves off the hook because things get uncomfortable. Ted Sizer said, "The students are watching." So let's model for them how to speak up around what matters.

THE CONVERSATION CONTINUES . . .

Building Leadership Capacity in Schools by Linda Lambert, Association for Supervision & Curriculum Development, 1998

Leadership Capacity for Lasting School Improvement by Linda Lambert, Association for Supervision & Curriculum Development, 2003

Resource

Inspirational Quotes for Having Hard Conversations

Silence remains, inescapably, a form of speech.

—Susan Sontag

Never grow a wishbone . . . where your backbone ought to be.

—Clementine Paddleford

Life shrinks or expands in proportion to one's courage.

—Anaïs Nin

Make it your business to share your truth, make it your listener's business to deal with his feelings.

—Molly Gordon

Strike when the iron is cold.

—Anonymous

We must become both hospice workers to support the peaceful dying and letting go of our traditional culture of fear and cynicism, and midwives to gently usher in our emerging culture of trust and mutual regard.

—Former CA State Assemblyman John Vasconcellos

Get into trouble, necessary trouble.

—U.S. Congressman John Lewis

If you think adventure is dangerous, try routine. It's lethal.

—Paulo Coehlo

Voyages are accomplished inwardly, and the most hazardous ones, needless to say, are made without moving from the spot.

—Henry Miller

Never, never be afraid to do what's right, especially if the well-being of a person or an animal is at stake. Society's punishments are small compared to the wounds we inflict on our soul when we look the other way.

—Reverend Martin Luther King

I have come to believe . . . that what is most important to me must be spoken, made verbal and shared, even at the risk of having it bruised or misunderstood . . . Your silence will not protect you . . . For we have been socialized to respect fear more than our own needs for language and definition, and while we wait in silence for that final luxury of fearlessness, the weight of that silence will choke us.

—Audre Lorde

The truth will set you free, but first it will piss you off.

—Gloria Steinem

Be the change you wish to see in the world.

—Mahatma Gandhi

You cannot plough a field by turning it over in your mind.

—Anonymous

Well-behaved women seldom make history.

—Laurel Thatcher Ulrich

Put on your big girl underpants and deal.

—Anonymous

Suppress, repress, depress, or express. You choose. When we do not "speak into" that which rises in us and we rather compress the energy internally, it eventually does one of the above. Until we express, the energy is not free, and neither are we. Lean into it. You'll choose wisely.

—Dr. Sue Morter

Yesterday I was clever and tried to change the world. Today I am wise and try to change myself.

—Rumi

I know that incivility is immoral and dangerous to democracy. People of faith in particular are called to speak and act on the assumption of shared human dignity. This does not rule out vigorous disagreement, but it forbids the cultivation of contempt and the issuing of threats.

—Michael Gerson

References and Suggested Readings

Abrams, J. (2009). *Having hard conversations.* Thousand Oaks, CA: Corwin.

Abrams, J., & von Frank, V. (2013). *The multigenerational workplace: Communicate, collaborate, & create community.* Thousand Oaks, CA: Corwin.

Ashford, S. J., & Detert, J. (2015). Get the boss to buy in. *Harvard Business Review,* January/February 2015.

Berger, J. G. (2013). *Changing on the job: Developing leaders for a complex world.* Stanford, CA: Stanford Business Books.

Brett, J., Behfar, K., & Sanchez-Burks, J. (2013, December 4). How to argue across cultures. *Harvard Business Review* Blog Network. Retrieved from http://blogs.hbr.org/2013/12/how-to-argue-across-cultures/

Bryk, A., & Schneider, B. (2002). *Trust in schools: A core resource for improvement* (American Sociological Association's Rose Series in Sociology). New York: Russell Sage Foundation.

Center for Compassion and Altruism Research and Education (n.d.). Stanford School of Medicine. Retrieved from http://ccare.stanford.edu/tag/ccare/

Cohen, A. R., & Bradford, D. (2012). *Influencing up.* Hoboken, NJ: Wiley.

Costa, A., & Garmston, R. (2002). *Cognitive coaching: A foundation for renaissance schools* (2nd ed.). Norwood, MA: Christopher-Gordon Publishers.

Costa, A., Garmston, R., with Ellison, J., & Hayes, C. (2015). *Cognitive coaching: Developing self-directed leaders and learners* (3rd ed.). Lanham, MD: Rowman & Littlefield.

Cuddy, A. (2012, June). Amy Cuddy: Your body language shapes who you are [Video file]. Retrieved from http://www.ted.com/talks/amy_cuddy_your_body_language_shapes_who_you_are.html

Davidson, R., with Begley, S. (2002). *The emotional life of your brain: How its unique patterns affect the way you think, feel and live—and how you can change them.* New York: Hudson Street Press.

Drago-Severson, E. (2009). *Leading adult learning: Supporting adult development in our schools.* Thousand Oaks, CA: Corwin.

Drago-Severson, E., & Blum-DeStefano, J. (2013). *Learning for leadership: Developmental strategies for building capacity in our schools.* Thousand Oaks, CA: Corwin.

Drago-Severson, E., & Blum-DeStefano, J. (2014). Tell me so I can hear: A developmental approach to feedback and collaboration. *JSD,* December 2014.

Dweck, C. (2007). *Mindset: The new psychology of success.* New York: Ballantine.

Freedman, M. (2013, October 8). How do you manage up in the workplace? *Insights,* Stanford Graduate School of Business. Retrieved from http://www.gsb.stanford.edu/insights/david-l-bradford-how-do-you-manage-workplace

Fullan, M. (2007). *Leading in a culture of change.* San Francisco, CA: Jossey-Bass.

Garmston, R. (2012). *Unlocking group potential to improve schools.* Thousand Oaks, CA: Corwin.

Garmston, R., & Costa, A. L. (2015). *Cognitive coaching: Developing self-directed leaders and learners.* Lanham, MD: Rowan & Littlefield.

Garmston, R., & Wellman, B. (1999). *The adaptive school: A sourcebook for developing collaborative groups.* Norwood, MA: Christopher-Gordon Publishers.

Garmston, R., & Zimmerman, D. P. (2013). *Lemons to lemonade: Resolving problems in meetings, workshops, and PLCS.* Thousand Oaks, CA: Corwin.

Gordon, D. T. (2002). Fuel for reform: The importance of trust in changing schools. *Harvard Education Letter, 8*(4).

Goulston, M. (2013, November 15). Don't get defensive: Communication tips for the vigilant. *Harvard Business Review* Blog Network. Retrieved from http://blogs.hbr.org/2013/11/dont-get-defensive-communication-tips-for-the-vigilant/

Goulston, M. (2015, June 3). How do you know if you talk too much? *Harvard Business Review* Blog Network. Retrieved from https://hbr.org/2015/06/how-to-know-if-you-talk-too-much/.

Greater Good Science Center. (n.d.) University of California, Berkeley. Retrieved from http://greatergood.berkeley.edu/

Gruenfeld, D. H. (2013). Power & influence [Video file]. Retrieved from http://leanin.org/education/power-influence/

Haidt, J. (2013). *The righteous mind: Why good people are divided by politics and religion.* New York: Vintage.

Hargreaves, A., & Fullan, M. (2012). *Professional capital: Transforming teaching in every school.* New York: Teachers College Press.

Heath, C., & Heath, D. (2010). *Switch: How to change things when change is hard.* New York: Broadway Books.

Heen, S., & Stone, D. (2014). Find the coaching in criticism. *Harvard Business Review Magazine,* January–February 2014. Retrieved from http://hbr.org/2014/01/find-the-coaching-in-criticism/ar/1

Kay, K., & Shipman, C. (2014). The confidence gap. *The Atlantic,* May 2014. Retrieved from http://www.theatlantic.com/magazine/archive/2014/05/the-confidence-gap/359815/

Kegan, R., & Lahey, L. L. (2001*). How the way we talk can change the way we work: Seven languages for transformation.* San Francisco, CA: Jossey-Bass.

Kegan, R., & Lahey, L. L. (2009). *Immunity to change: How to overcome it and unlock the potential in yourself and your organization.* Boston, MA: Harvard Business Review Press.

Kets de Vries, M. F. R. (2014). Coaching the toxic leader. *Harvard Business Review,* April 2014. Retrieved from https://hbr.org/2014/04/coaching-the-toxic-leader/ar/1

Kise, J. A. G. (2014). *Unleashing the positive power of differences: Polarity thinking in our schools.* Thousand Oaks, CA: Corwin.

Kitroeff, N. (2015). Five strange workplace conversation tips from a hostage negotiator. Retrieved from http://www.bloomberg.com/news/articles/2015-03-30/five-strange-workplace-conversation-tips-from-a-hostage-negotiator

Lambert, L. (1998). *Building leadership capacity in schools.* Alexandria, VA: Association for Supervision & Curriculum Development.

Lambert, L. (2003). *Leadership capacity for lasting school improvement.* Alexandria, VA: Association for Supervision & Curriculum Development.

Lerner, H. (2001). *The dance of connection: How to talk to someone when you're mad, hurt, scared, frustrated, insulted, betrayed or desperate.* New York: HarperCollins.

Lerner, H. (2005). *The dance of fear: Rising above anxiety, fear, and shame to be your best and bravest self.* New York: HarperCollins.

Lieberman, M. D. (2013). *Social: Why our brains are wired to connect.* New York: Crown Publishers.

Lipton, L., & Wellman, B. (2013). *Learning-focused supervision: Developing professional expertise in standards-driven systems.* Arlington, MA: MiraVia.

Maraboli, S. (n.d.). Dr. Steve Maraboli [Web site]. Retrieved from http://www.stevemaraboli.com/Motivational-Quotes.html

Markus, H. R., & Conner, A. (2014). *Clash!: How to thrive in a multicultural world.* New York: Plume.

Marshak, R. (2006). *Covert processes at work: Managing the five hidden dimensions of organizational change.* San Francisco, CA: Berrett-Koehler Publishers.

McLaren, K. (2010). *The language of emotions: What your feelings are trying to tell you.* Boulder, CO: Sounds True.

Meyer, E. (2014). *The culture map: Breaking through the invisible boundaries of global business.* Philadelphia, PA: Public Affairs.

Neff, K. (2011). *Self-compassion: The proven power of being kind to yourself.* New York: William Morrow.

O'Hara, M., & Leicester, G. (2012). *Dancing at the edge: Competence, culture and organization in the 21st century.* Scotland: International Futures Forum.

Palmer, P. J. (1998). *The courage to teach: Exploring the inner landscape of a teacher's life.* San Francisco, CA: Jossey-Bass.

Patterson, K., Grenny, J., McMillan, R., Switzler, A., & Maxfield, D. (2013). *Crucial accountability: Tools for resolving violated expectations, broken commitments, and bad behavior* (2nd ed.). New York: VitalSmarts.

Rock, D. (2008). SCARF: A brain-based model for collaborating with and influencing others. *NeuroLeadership Journal.* Retrieved from http://www.davidrock.net/files/NLJ_SCARFUS.pdf

Rock, D. (2009). *Your brain at work: Strategies for overcoming distraction, regaining focus, and working smarter all day long.* New York: Harper Business.

Sandberg, S. (2013). *Lean in: Women, work, and the will to lead.* New York: Knopf.

Schein, E. H. (2009). *Helping: How to offer, give, and receive help.* San Francisco, CA: Berrett-Koehler.

Schein, E. H. (2013). *Humble inquiry: The gentle art of asking instead of telling.* San Francisco, CA: Berrett-Koehler.

Schwartz, S. H. (2006). Basic human values: Theory, methods, and applications. Retrieved from http://yourmorals.org/schwartz.2006.basic%20human%20values.pdf

Seligman, M. (2006). *Learned optimism: How to change your mind and your life.* New York: Vintage.

Singleton, G. E., & Linton, C. (2006). *Courageous conversations about race: A field guide for achieving equity in schools.* Thousand Oaks, CA: Corwin.

Sternberg, R. (2002). *Why smart people can be so stupid.* New York: Oxford University Press.

Stone, D., & Heen, S. (2014). *Thanks for the feedback: The science and art of receiving feedback well.* New York: Viking/Penguin.

Victor Elementary School District. (2005). Basics. Retrieved from http://vesd-ca .schoolloop.com/file/1397284892362/1397283754073/8806528680096465 402.pdf

Wellman, B., & Lipton, L. (2004). *Data-driven dialogue: A facilitator's guide to collaborative inquiry.* Arlington, MA: MiraVia.

Zoller, K., & Landry, C. (2010). *The choreography of presenting: The 7 essential attributes of effective presenters.* Thousand Oaks, CA: Corwin.

Index

A SAGE Company

CORWIN HAS ONE MISSION: to enhance education through intentional professional learning.

We build long-term relationships with our authors, educators, clients, and associations who partner with us to develop and continuously improve the best evidence-based practices that establish and support lifelong learning.

THE PROFESSIONAL LEARNING ASSOCIATION

Learning Forward is a nonprofit, international membership association of learning educators committed to one vision in K–12 education: Excellent teaching and learning every day. To realize that vision, Learning Forward pursues its mission to build the capacity of leaders to establish and sustain highly effective professional learning. Information about membership, services, and products is available from www.learningforward.org.

Solutions you want. Experts you trust. Results you need.

AUTHOR CONSULTING

Author Consulting

On-site professional learning with sustainable results! Let us help you design a professional learning plan to meet the unique needs of your school or district. www.corwin.com/pd

INSTITUTES

Institutes

Corwin Institutes provide collaborative learning experiences that equip your team with tools and action plans ready for immediate implementation. www.corwin.com/institutes

ECOURSES

eCourses

Practical, flexible online professional learning designed to let you go at your own pace. www.corwin.com/ecourses

READ2EARN

Read2Earn

Did you know you can earn graduate credit for reading this book? Find out how: www.corwin.com/read2earn

Contact an account manager at (800) 831-6640 or visit **www.corwin.com** for more information.